THELMA & LOUISE

## REEL WEST

ANDREW PATRICK NELSON, SERIES EDITOR

Reel West is a unique series of short, neatly packaged
volumes exploring individual Western films across the whole
history of the canon, from early and classic Westerns to
revisionist and spaghetti Westerns. The series considers the
many themes and variations that have accrued over more
than a century of this most American of film styles. Intended
for general readers as well as for classroom use, these brief
books will offer smart, incisive examinations of the aesthetic,
cultural, experiential, and personal meaning and legacy of
the films they discuss and will provide strong arguments for
their importance—all filtered through the consciousness
of writers of distinction from within the disciplines of film
criticism, journalism, and literature.

Also available in the Reel West series:

*Ride Lonesome* by Kirk Ellis
*Blood on the Moon* by Alan K. Rode

# THELMA & LOUISE

### SUSAN KOLLIN

University of New Mexico Press ∩ Albuquerque

© 2023 by Susan Kollin
All rights reserved. Published 2023
Printed in the United States of America

ISBN 978-0-8263-6552-1 (paper)
ISBN 978-0-8263-6553-8 (electronic)
Library of Congress Cataloging-in-Publication data is on file with
    the Library of Congress

Founded in 1889, the University of New Mexico sits on the traditional homelands
of the Pueblo of Sandia. The original peoples of New Mexico—Pueblo, Navajo, and
Apache—since time immemorial have deep connections to the land and have made
significant contributions to the broader community statewide. We honor the land
itself and those who remain stewards of this land throughout the generations and
also acknowledge our committed relationship to Indigenous peoples. We gratefully
recognize our history.

Cover illustration: Still from *Thelma & Louise*
Designed by Felicia Cedillos
Composed in Adobe Jenson 9.25/13.75

# CONTENTS

List of Illustrations / vii

Acknowledgments / ix

Introduction / 1

1. | Gender, Sexuality, and the Western / 9

2. | "A Love Letter to the West" / 39

3. | "We're Fugitives Now": Women, Guns, and Violence / 63

Conclusion. | Beyond the Abyss / 93

Notes / 101

Bibliography / 111

# ILLUSTRATIONS

Figure 1. Two friends getting ready for a weekend trip in *Thelma & Louise* (1991) / 4

Figure 2. Introducing the gun and the popular Western in *Thelma & Louise* (1991) / 13

Figure 3. Going out in a blaze of glory in *Butch Cassidy and the Sundance Kid* (1969) / 14

Figure 4. Driving over the edge in *Thelma & Louise* (1991) / 14

Figure 5. Dancing at the Silver Bullet bar in *Thelma & Louise* (1991) / 17

Figure 6. Louise dresses Western in *Thelma & Louise* (1991) / 17

Figure 7. J. D., the cowboy drifter, amid the tumbleweeds in *Thelma & Louise* (1991) / 19

Figure 8. A cattle drive in *Thelma & Louise* (1991) / 19

Figure 9. Jimmy and his horse lamp in *Thelma & Louise* (1991) / 20

Figure 10. Hal and his horse sculpture in *Thelma & Louise* (1991) / 21

Figure 11. Spouting water as phallic imagery in *Thelma & Louise* (1991) / 23

Figure 12. Pumping iron in *Thelma & Louise* (1991) / 23

Figure 13. Pumping oil in *Thelma & Louise* (1991) / 23

Figure 14. Texaco and 76 signs in *Thelma & Louise* (1991) / 27

Figure 15. Texaco sign as a traumatic reminder of the past in *Thelma & Louise* (1991) / 27

Figure 16. Louise as a 1940s Hollywood actress in
  *Thelma & Louise* (1991) / 34

Figure 17. J. D. poses as an outlaw in *Thelma & Louise* (1991) / 42

Figure 18. The western landscape of *Thelma & Louise* (1991) / 48

Figure 19. Escaping the law in *Badlands* (1973) / 49

Figure 20. The modern West of *Badlands* (1973) / 49

Figure 21. Louise holds a gun to Harlan's head in
  *Thelma & Louise* (1991) / 67

Figure 22. Vienna, the female gunslinger and saloon owner in
  *Johnny Guitar* (1954) / 72

Figure 23. Gunslinger Jessica with her firearm in
  *Forty Guns* (1957) / 74

Figure 24. Belle Starr, a spaghetti Western gunslinger in
  *The Belle Starr Story* (1968) / 75

Figure 25. Thomas mansplains how to shoot a gun in
  *Hannie Caulder* (1971) / 76

Figure 26. Darryl gaslights in *Thelma & Louise* (1991) / 80

Figure 27. Thelma takes aim at a police officer in
  *Thelma & Louise* (1991) / 82

Figure 28. Teaching manners to a truck driver in
  *Thelma & Louise* (1991) / 85

Figure 29. African American cyclist in *Thelma & Louise* (1991) / 88

Figure 30. Native American diners in *Thelma & Louise* (1991) / 89

Figure 31. Exchanging jewelry for a hat in *Thelma & Louise* (1991) / 90

Figure 32. The carbon footprint of *Thelma & Louise* (1991) / 91

Figure 33. Velma and Lucy on the road in *Smoke Signals* (1998) / 96

Figure 34. Female gunslingers in *Bandidas* (2006) / 98

# ACKNOWLEDGMENTS

Scholarship is never a solitary act but comes into being in the context of community and through a writer's connections and interactions with other people. I have thus incurred many debts in the process of completing this book. First, I would like to thank Andrew Patrick Nelson for inviting me to contribute to the Reel West series for the University of New Mexico Press. I especially appreciate his trust and patience when the COVID-19 pandemic so completely rerouted my attention and commitments, as well as his help with the images here. Thanks also to Stephen Hull at the University of New Mexico Press for his advice, care, and guidance in the process of completing this book. I also wish to thank the anonymous reviewers for their helpful comments, and Marie Landau, James Ayers, and Anna Pohlod for their editorial assistance.

The Office of the Provost at Montana State University (MSU) funded a sabbatical leave that allowed me to work on this book. At MSU, I have had the incredible support of colleagues, friends, and students who have helped me clarify the arguments I make here. As my primary scholarly home for many years, the Western Literature Association (WLA) has also supported me in numerous ways. In particular, members of the organization have helped me develop my thinking on gender, race, ecology, belonging, care, refusal, and the Western. At MSU and the WLA, I especially wish to acknowledge Dan Flory, Melody Graulich, Nancy Cook, Steve Tatum, Robert Bennett, Liza Nicholas, Mary Murphy, Bob Rydell, Susan Bernardin, Neil Campbell, Cindy Stillwell, Alex Harmon, Matt Herman, Susan Cohen, Kristen Intemann, Christine Bold, Victoria Lamont, Krista Comer, José Aranda, Audrey Goodman, Bill Handley, Kirby Brown, Lisa Tatonetti, Gretchen Minton, Marvin Lansverk, Linda Karell, Amanda Hendrix-Komoto, Rebecca Lush, Kalenda Eaton, Michael K. Johnson, Chad Allen, Alex Young, and Sabine Barcatta.

Dan Flory read the entire book while he was completing his own projects on philosophy and the Western. I am grateful to him for the valuable comments and insights he provided, in addition to his love and intellectual support over the years. I also wish to thank the undergraduate and graduate students in my classes on the Western, feminism, race, and the environmental humanities for helping me see how these topics and concerns inform each other in meaningful and sometimes unexpected ways.

Thanks to my sister for our road trips and for all the driving. Over the years, longtime friends Tina and Art have shared my love of film and television. Their care, generosity, and good food have made my academic and life journeys through the North and the West such a pleasure. Finally, I wish to express love and gratitude to my daughters for teaching me how feminism changes and evolves, lives on and thrives. This book is dedicated to them.

# Introduction

With a script by first-time screenwriter Callie Khouri and under the direction of filmmaker Ridley Scott, *Thelma & Louise* was an unexpected hit when it was released in the summer of 1991. The film had a relatively modest budget of less than $17 million, but it ended up grossing more than $45 million at the box office, well beyond what studio heads had initially anticipated. The movie premiered at Cannes film festival as its closing title and went on to earn a Golden Globe (Best Screenplay—Motion Picture), Oscar (Best Original Screenplay), and Writers Guild of America Award (Best Original Screenplay). *Thelma & Louise* likewise won the London Critics' Circle Film Award for Director of the Year and Film of the Year, and it earned additional nominations and awards from other film organizations. Currently, the Writers Guild of America West places *Thelma & Louise* at number 71 on its list of best screenplays, while the American Film Institute ranks the movie's main female characters at number 24 on its list of top heroes in cinema. In 2016, the Library of Congress selected the movie for preservation in the National Film Registry, and in summer 2021, plans were announced about the development of a new *Thelma & Louise* musical.[1]

In the more than three decades since it appeared in theaters, *Thelma*

& *Louise* has remained an influential film that continues to attract discussion and debate about its treatment of violence and retribution, gender and sexuality, and the changing meanings of the American West. The movie tells the story of two friends who become unlikely criminals after they flee a murder scene and travel across the West, hoping to make it to Mexico, where they can escape the law. The film features not one but two female leads who refuse to settle for less and instead fight back against sexual assault and harassment, wielding guns while having each other's back. As a blockbuster that garnered numerous awards, *Thelma & Louise* contributed to the revisionist cycle of the Western that began in the early 1990s after *Dances with Wolves* (Kevin Costner, 1990) swept the Oscars. Viewers often lament that Westerns seemed to fade away after the "golden age" of the genre—roughly the 1930s to the 1960s—when one-quarter of all Hollywood films produced were Westerns.[2] Yet concerns about the decline in numbers can be a problem, as Andrew Patrick Nelson points out, because they obscure how recent years have actually seen the production of a "remarkable *variety* of film and television Westerns," many of which center on groups previously marginalized by the genre.[3]

As a feminist revisionist Western, *Thelma & Louise* was shaped by particular commitments and influences. Khouri began writing the screenplay in 1988, the same year that *The Accused* (Jonathan Kaplan) was released, a film that centers on the brutal gang rape of a woman (Jodie Foster) and her struggles for justice. That movie inspired tremendous critical and popular attention and also went on to win a number of awards, including a Golden Globe and an Oscar for Foster's performance. The success of *The Accused* helped pave the way for *Thelma & Louise*, which also explores gender, power, and sexuality while offering a different take on the Western.[4]

*Thelma & Louise* hit theaters in the summer of 1991, just two weeks after William Kennedy Smith was charged with raping a woman in Palm Beach. That fall, Clarence Thomas was confirmed as a justice of the Supreme Court after Anita Hill gave testimony that he sexually harassed her in the workplace. Likewise, the day before the film was released, the Supreme Court ruled that it was constitutional to restrict federally funded clinics from offering information to patients about abortion.[5] That year also saw the publication of Susan Faludi's book *Backlash*, a best-selling study about the media's attack on feminism, which sparked its own intense debates about the treatment of gender, sexuality, and politics in the popular press.[6] *Thelma & Louise* entered these larger conversations, developing a plot informed by feminism that highlights the importance of female friendships, support, and love as a means of survival. The film addresses the gendered politics of mobility, following two friends who engage in unsanctioned escape from their domestic lives and relationships with men.[7] In doing so, *Thelma & Louise* features different kinds of outlaws in the West and foregrounds the challenges they face in seeking justice in a male-dominated world.

From the time it was released, *Thelma & Louise* has been classified across a number of genres, including the road movie, the buddy film, the screwball comedy, the action-adventure movie, as well as the Western. In Hollywood, filmmakers often combine or mix genres in order to innovate the art and to expand the potential audience for a movie, ensuring it has a strong return at the box office.[8] Khouri's script, shaped by a certain set of political and artistic allegiances, challenges popular genres and reroutes their plots and conflicts for new pleasures. *Thelma & Louise* thus uses the journey of two unlikely renegades to explore ideas about freedom and the search for identity and meaning, centering on the rebellions and struggles

Figure 1. Two friends getting ready for a weekend trip in *Thelma & Louise* (1991)

of its lead female characters in order to develop new stories about the West.

In her study *Hooked: Art and Attachment*, critic Rita Felski examines the strong and often passionate responses that the movie inspired among viewers. She argues that some of the power of *Thelma & Louise* as a cultural text may found in how it "did not simply speak to preexisting groups but called these groups into being." As Felski points out, viewers often "defined themselves as fans or skeptics, as antifeminist or as subscribing to differing kinds of feminism" and frequently "came to see themselves as part of a 'we,'" as a "virtual feminist community founded in devotion to a film and what it stood for."[9] As such, *Thelma & Louise* helped create a "feminist counter-public sphere," what Felski defines as a "space of public debate about newly compelling and contentious topics." Raising questions about gender politics, sexuality, harassment, and cultural representation, the film had a tremendous social and political impact that may still be recognized today, even as there are some limitations in this regard.[10]

*Thelma & Louise* is an important and complicated film to include in in the University of New Mexico Press's Reel West series. While one could focus on other significant "women's Westerns" from the genre's golden age or an example from the more recent crop of revisionist Westerns appearing on television and the big screen, few titles seem to have achieved the level of cultural influence that *Thelma & Louise* managed to attain over the years. Today when we speak of someone "driving over the cliff," for instance, the phrase may resonate in ways similar to phrases from earlier classic Westerns, such as "That'll be the day," a refrain John Wayne made throughout *The Searchers* (John Ford, 1956) or "When you call me that, smile!," a statement that Gary Cooper didn't quite say in *The Virginian* (Victor Fleming, 1929) but that helped build the reputation of the movie and Westerns in general.

Over the years, *Thelma & Louise* has entered the popular imagination, with parodies and references to its plot and characters appearing in hit television shows such as *The Simpsons*, *Seinfeld*, and *Family Guy*, to name just a few examples. In addition to these cultural references, a number of academic and popular books devoted to the movie have been published since its release, including Marita Sturken's *Thelma & Louise* (2000; revised 2020), Bernie Cook's edited collection *Thelma & Louise Live! The Cultural Afterlife of an American Film* (2007), and Becky Aikman's *Off the Cliff: How the Making of Thelma & Louise Drove Hollywood to the Edge* (2017). Likewise, various magazines and journals have featured special issues or cover stories about the film, including *Newsweek*, *Film Quarterly*, and *Cineaste*.

As many critics note, the Western is a capacious and shifting genre that is able to serve a number of diverse purposes and pleasures.[11] Featuring white female outlaws struggling against different types of violence and "savagery" in the form of sexism and misogyny, *Thelma & Louise* enters the contested terrain of the American West, extending the genre's typical cast of heroes and villains as well as its standard plots and themes. Chapter 1, "Gender, Sexuality, and the Western," addresses how the film portrays the American West as a complex region that poses obstacles for the main characters as they embark on their escape. In doing so, the chapter explores how the movie treats freedom, independence, and self-reliance, concepts that often shape the Western and that are central to dominant understandings of American national identity. While the two women in the film may strive to achieve mainstream ideals of freedom and self-reliance, these qualities appear elusive or unavailable to them, or as less than useful to their attempts to survive. Offering a close analysis of *Thelma & Louise* as a Western, this chapter examines how the film relies on and extends aspects of the genre while employing a feminist perspective that complicates ideas about Western freedom, independence, belonging, and community.

When *Thelma & Louise* opened, audiences often disagreed about how to regard the white female leads—whether they should be understood as justice-bringing heroes or unredemptive villains who unleash antisocial forms of violence. The movie provoked powerful and intense reactions, particularly concerning its use of force, its critique of white male power and entitlement, and its revisions of the Western genre. Chapter 2, "'A Love Letter to the West,'" restores to memory the contributions that women from a variety of backgrounds made to the genre while examining *Thelma & Louise* in the context of film history. Although the Western is commonly recognized as a male-centered tradition, I join other feminist scholars who note problems in overstating this claim, particularly because it risks erasing the long history of women who shaped the genre's development in their capacity as writers, directors, producers, and performers.

In this chapter, I also examine how *Thelma & Louise* generated enormous controversy, particularly regarding changing ideas about gender, sexuality, and power, as well as shifting ideas about America and the West.

Over the years, the Western has also been recognized as a white settler genre, a point that few would argue with but if overstated can be misleading. Critics must be careful not to obscure the important contributions of racially diverse artists, including Native American performers and filmmakers who made Westerns and movies about the West, from the earliest days of cinema, that work against the grain of the genre. These films foreground how the Western can be reimagined in ways that counter settler myths and fantasies and offer more truthful and engaging stories about Indigenous struggles for sovereignty. Noting this work, I examine how race often seems to be an unmarked category in *Thelma & Louise* but actually shapes various elements of the story and underwrites crucial events in the film.

Chapter 3, "'We're Fugitives Now': Women, Guns, and Violence," traces how *Thelma & Louise* became a powerful reference point for discussions about sexual consent, rebellion against restrictive gender roles, and the place of violence in struggles for social change. In this discussion, I avoid using narrow definitions of violence and instead recognize how the concept operates on many levels, as both a physical and an ideological or political force. The chapter builds on recent writing about epistemology and ethics developed by feminist philosophers who emphasize diverse ways of knowing while also addressing epistemic violence and injustice— the conflicts that may arise in producing knowledge about difference and identity. From these discussions, viewers may recognize how *Thelma & Louise* takes up important feminist critiques about silence, erasure, and gaslighting while also addressing forms of protest and rebellion that have emerged to counter these problems.

In many ways, *Thelma & Louise* became a key text for both recent Westerns and feminist films. The conclusion, "Beyond the Abyss," examines how *Thelma & Louise* continues to exert influence in movies and television by opening up new avenues for the Western and by sparking new interest in plots involving overlooked or marginalized groups. The movie also marked a turning point for cinematic discussions about power, revenge, and critiques of gender privilege. It is difficult to imagine, for instance, that a recent show like *Unbelievable* (created by Susannah Grant, Ayelet Waldman, and Michael Chabon, 2019) or a film such as *Promising Young Woman* (Emerald Fennell, 2020) could have been made without *Thelma & Louise*.

In this way, the movie is fascinating to examine for how it encouraged larger discussions and conversations about acceptable responses to sexual violence and injustice. Disappointment and rage shape the action of the film, responses that are often treated ambivalently in mainstream American culture. While it provides a means for addressing these emotions, *Thelma & Louise* also offers love and friendship in ways that suggest additional routes for achieving social change. Ultimately, the film points to the manner in which transgressive emotions like anger, rage, and disillusionment, alongside other feelings such as care and affection, may serve as important tools for surviving flawed relationships, restrictive social norms, and challenging life journeys as depicted in the Western. It is important to note too that the film contains flaws that must be addressed. These problems include the treatment of racist symbols, settler colonialism, whiteness, and ecology, all of which are political concerns that have reshaped the genre of the Western in the many years since *Thelma & Louise* first appeared.

# 1. | Gender, Sexuality, and the Western

n a 2015 panel on screenwriting hosted by the Austin Film Festival, Callie Khouri described her experiences working on the script for *Thelma & Louise*. "The whole feeling of the movie came at once. It was like getting punched in the heart," she said. "I knew the ending, so I just had to figure out where to start."[1] As she forged ahead and completed her screenplay, Khouri encountered the next steps in getting the film made. Working as an assistant for a production company in Los Angeles at the time, she recognized many of the pitfalls that can impede the process, especially for women writers. "I thought, 'They'll give me $5,000, tell me how lucky I am, give it to some director, change it, and then I'll be even more pissed off than I already am.'"[2] Although Khouri was a first-time writer, her script managed to get the green light and went on to evoke a tremendous response upon its release. While her experiences in production helped prepare her for some of the challenges of moviemaking, Khouri confessed she had not anticipated how the film would capture the cultural moment and had no idea that the movie would "stick around as long as it has."[3]

*Thelma & Louise* tells the story of two friends from Arkansas who plan a lighthearted trip to a lakeside cabin for a few days of fishing and fun. The purpose of their trip is to take a temporary break from a stifling marriage, in the case of Thelma (Geena Davis), and a dead-end job, in the case of Louise (Susan Sarandon). Shortly after their adventure begins, they decide to stop at a roadhouse—named, significantly, the Silver Bullet—for a quick drink before heading to the cabin. At the bar, Thelma dances with a man named Harlan (Timothy Carhart) who plies her with alcohol and then lures her to the parking lot, where he tries to rape her. Gun in hand, Louise confronts the man, pressing the muzzle against the side of his head and threatening to shoot him if he doesn't stop. Harlan backs off, and Thelma is able to escape. As the women return to their car, Harlan yells that he should have raped Thelma after all and then goes on to taunt Louise, who reacts in anger and shoots the man dead.

Thelma and Louise quickly flee the crime scene. Now outlaws, they decide to head to Mexico, a location where many bandits in Western movies have fled. Beginning in the silent era, as Christopher Frayling notes, US filmmakers have often presented Mexico as a space of retreat, a place for Anglo heroes to locate "lost ideals," and an imagined terrain that provides an "exotic alternative" from the restrictions shaping their lives north of the border.[4] Instead of traveling directly to Mexico, however, Louise insists on taking a route that will keep them out of Texas. As she explains, "Look, you shoot off a guy's head with his pants down, believe me, Texas is the not the place you want to get caught." When Thelma questions her about Texas, Louise responds forcefully, making it clear she's trying to avoid a terrifying memory from her past. "It happened to you, didn't it?" Thelma asks her. "Just drop it, we're not going to talk about it," Louise snaps back. The mood shifts at this point, with Louise's quick outburst followed by silence, providing an important but unspoken backstory that helps explain why she fired the fatal shot into Harlan.

Meanwhile, Hal Slocumb (Harvey Keitel), a sympathetic lawman back in Arkansas, becomes involved in the murder investigation. Although he tries to help the women return safely to face the charges against them, their situation quickly spirals out of control, particularly after they meet a sexy cowboy drifter named J. D. (Bratt Pitt) who feels entitled to Louise's life savings, steals her pile of money, and upends their means for escape. The women's problems escalate further after Thelma decides to replace the stolen money by robbing a convenience store, using the script she learned from J. D. in the motel room the previous night.

Later the two women lock a police officer in the trunk of his patrol car after he pulls them over for speeding, thus adding to their growing list of offenses. Toward the end of the film, the crime spree continues, with Thelma and Louise becoming vengeful gunslingers who partake in a dramatic act of vigilante justice by blowing up a fuel tanker after its driver refuses to apologize for his lewd and offensive behavior. In a final showdown with police who manage to catch up with the women as they approach the Grand Canyon, the female outlaws decide they will not surrender. Vowing to keep going, Thelma and Louise drive over the cliff together, holding hands as their car flies past the edge, in what has become one of Hollywood's most dramatic and memorable endings.

While many audience members were surprised and dismayed by the closing scene, with some viewers feeling angry and betrayed, early moments in the film foreshadow problems that lead up to the fateful conclusion. When we first meet Thelma, she is at home waiting for her husband Darryl (Christopher McDonald) to head off to work before getting ready for her trip with Louise. Once he leaves, Thelma races through her bedroom, finding items to take on their weekend getaway. She isn't sure what to pack and hedges her bets by throwing in more than she would need for a short weekend trip. Watching Thelma with her overpacked bags, viewers may be left wondering if she ever meant to return home in the first place. By keeping the trip secret from Darryl and later leaving him a frozen meal and a warm beer near the microwave for dinner, Thelma's actions indicate that she may already be plotting a break from her oppressive marriage. Perhaps Hal the law officer is right when he says it looks like she wasn't planning to return anytime soon.

In a meaningful sequence, Thelma opens the drawer of a bedside table and comes across two items: a Western novel by popular author Tony Hillerman and Darryl's handgun. Thelma puts the firearm in her luggage, leaving the Western behind. The camera lingers over the gun, which Thelma gingerly places in her bag, while providing a glimpse of the book's cover. Fans of Hillerman may recognize the novel as part of the author's best-selling Navajo crime and detective series set in the Southwest. The volume pictured, A Thief of Time, tells the story of two law officers who track down a cold-blooded killer on the loose somewhere in the New Mexico desert. In this short sequence, the appearance of the gun and the brief reference to Hillerman's novel announces that we are entering the world of the Western. The scene also foreshadows later developments in the story when the two female characters face decisive moments of violence and conflict.

Thelma's decision to keep the novel in the drawer may resonate in other ways as well, perhaps signaling the screenwriter's effort to leave behind some aspects of the Western. In this way, Khouri's script foregrounds different routes for storytelling and different means of narrating women's experiences and struggles in the genre. This shift away from the popular Western

Figure 2. Introducing the gun and the popular Western in *Thelma & Louise* (1991)

appears near the end of the film, which recalls a similar scene in *Butch Cassidy and the Sundance Kid* (George Roy Hill, 1969) where the two heroes, surrounded by the Bolivian army, meet their fate in a blast of gunfire. In a meaningful way, the soundtracks that punctuate the end of the two films differ significantly. While in *Butch Cassidy and the Sundance Kid* the sound of gunshots firing into the outlaws then cuts to piano music that expresses a sense of loss and the end of adventure, *Thelma & Louise* uses soaring, uplifting notes that suggest triumph and possibility even as the two women drive into the abyss. The final scene is followed by a montage featuring moments of their life together that plays throughout the credits. *Thelma & Louise* does not show the female characters being dramatically killed off but instead leaves them suspended in midair, an image that for Khouri suggests potential other futures rather than death and suicide.

This much-debated scene left some viewers dissatisfied. In her review for the *Los Angeles Times*, for instance, Sheila Benson argued that the film was just a rehash of movies like *Smokey and the Bandit* (1977), with a "downbeat ending" that provided little by way of entertainment, even with

Figure 3. Going out in a blaze of glory in *Butch Cassidy and the Sundance Kid* (1969)

Figure 4. Driving over the edge in *Thelma & Louise* (1991)

a woman "at the wheel."⁵ Yet if placed within the context of the genre, the ending sequence takes on new significance. In the logic of the Western, characters who have engaged in violence are often unable to return to society—such brutality places them outside the social order, where they must move on and build a new life for themselves elsewhere, as we see in *The Searchers, Shane* (1953), and many other Westerns.

For female characters in the genre, additional problems also emerge.

Addressing gender in the Western, Pam Cook describes how women often manage to escape the confines of gender, only to become "rehabilitated" by the end of the story. In the Western, these wayward women are required to "relinquish" their position as "active and independent" figures and forced to accept a "secondary status" that entails giving their power over to the male hero. Cook notes that even when a female character somehow remains active in the Western, she often does so "in the hero's cause rather than her own."[6] In Khouri's script, the controversial ending forgoes this resolution by instead showcasing the women's rejection of and refusal to return to their previous lives, jobs, and relationships. Indeed, the only option for them is to keep moving forward and continue pushing against the roadblocks to discover what other options might await them. There is "no place" for them in their current lives, Khouri explained in a 1996 interview. "The world is not big enough to support them. They will be brought down if they stay here."[7] In that way, the final scene may be regarded as triumphant rather than tragic. It marks their refusal to return to the restricted and confining roles assigned to them in their everyday lives and in the logic of the Western. The ending instead signals their commitment to move on and their desire to explore other possibilities.

Khouri's efforts to open up opportunities for her main characters are hinted at in early scenes of the film. The beginning of the movie features a flash-forward that includes a black-and-white panorama of the Southwest landscape. Slowly, the faded shot morphs into color, a transformation reminiscent of a similar shift in *The Wizard of Oz* (Victor Fleming, 1939), when Dorothy leaves Kansas and arrives in a magical world full of color. References to the earlier film continue in the scene at the motel room, where Thelma asks J. D., "Who are you anyway?" and he playfully answers, "I am the great and powerful Oz." In many ways, the young cowboy drifter is indeed like the man behind the curtain, someone who offers false promises and is not what he appears to be. In *The Wizard of Oz*, the great and powerful man behind the curtain is something of a con artist who does not hold the power to rescue Dorothy and her friends. Neither do any of the male characters in *Thelma & Louise*. Instead, just as Dorothy discovers, Khouri's female characters have to take care of things themselves, relying on their own wits, and each other, to solve their problems.[8]

Similarly, the opening scene in *Thelma & Louise* signals a departure from the genre in its reversal of the closing shot in *Butch Cassidy and the Sundance Kid*. In the final sequence of the 1969 Western, the shot changes from full color to a faded sepia, suggesting that the lives of these male outlaws will soon become myth, that their history as bank robbers will be transformed into Western legend. Shifting in the other direction from black and white to full color, *Thelma & Louise* offers a different perspective, implying that the female protagonists are moving away from the gendered fantasies and myths that restricted their lives. The shift to color suggests a world beyond these gender limits and a move beyond the scripted roles of the Western, as the two female characters propel themselves into a new space of possibility.

*Thelma & Louise* employs other visual cues that foreground its relationship to the Western. In addition to the gun and Hillerman's novel, *Thelma & Louise* uses costume as a means of signaling the genre. At the Silver Bullet bar, many of the patrons wear Western-style clothing while dancing to country music that plays in the background. Even in scenes that are set in the South, the film gestures to the Western.[9] Harlan, J. D., and Jimmy (Louise's boyfriend, played by Michael Madsen), for instance, appear in Western-style shirts, boots, hats, or belts, while Thelma's and Louise's transformations are likewise mirrored in their clothing. Here the task of taking control of their lives requires each female lead to also take control of her body and its self-fashioning. In an early scene that shows her getting ready for the trip, for instance, Louise puts on a black, Western-style jacket with embroidered designs. The outfit suggests she's in search of fun and adventure, a look she will cast off later in the film. After she and Thelma flee the initial crime scene and take to the road, Louise encounters an old man sitting on a weathered bench at a gas station and trades her jewelry for his hat, thus indicating her desire to adopt a new identity. Now sporting faded blue jeans, a bandanna, a white T-shirt, and a well-worn cowboy hat, Louise is dressed for the business of survival in the West.

Figure 5. Dancing at the Silver Bullet bar in Thelma & Louise (1991)

Figure 6. Louise dresses Western in *Thelma & Louise* (1991)

Thelma's outfits undergo a similar transformation after she casts aside the frilly white shirt, ruffled skirt, and rhinestone jean jacket that she wears early in the film. Thelma dons Louise's cowgirl jacket later in the story and finally settles on her own outlaw clothing, which she wears through the ending of the film. Such transformation may be something of a rarity in the genre, as Pam Cook notes. Because many Westerns often work at "re-establishing sexual boundaries," she writes, "it's unusual for the woman who starts out wearing pants, carrying a gun and riding a horse to be still doing so at the end of the movie."[10] For Thelma, however, the transformation works in reverse—she begins the journey in a skirt but moves to wearing pants by the end of the film.

In *Thelma & Louise*, various exterior shots also establish genre, with the film's use of Southwest landscapes calling to mind similar desert locations often featured in the Western. Critic Josh Garrett-Davis discusses the power that popular Western movies often hold in shaping visual responses to the region and its art. He points out that the genre has "exerted" such a strong "cultural influence" that the landscape itself often ends up visually alluding to Westerns even when featured in other types of narratives or contexts.[11] With a few stock items, familiar characters, and the right backdrop, it can become difficult for stories to avoid being drawn into what Garrett-Davis calls the "orbit of the Western."[12] This complex interaction means that stories, film, and other artwork often end up utilizing a landscape that visually conjures up the Western genre, such that all of these entities become tangled together in complicated ways. In *Thelma & Louise*, genre is established through tumbleweeds that sweep across the dirt road in an early scene with the young hitchhiker J. D. and in another sequence involving cowboys on a cattle drive that the two women encounter on their escape through the back roads. Haunting Western guitar

Figure 7. J. D., the cowboy drifter, amid the tumbleweeds in *Thelma & Louise* (1991)

Figure 8. A cattle drive in *Thelma & Louise* (1991)

music composed by Hans Zimmer and other details in the production design likewise help situate the film in the world of the popular Western.

Interior shots also gesture toward the genre, including a scene show-casing details from Jimmy's home. Filmed by cinematographer Adrian Biddle, the scene uses dark lighting, but viewers are able to see some fur-niture, Jimmy's guitar, and a bucking bronco lamp that sits on his bed-side table. The visual references to the horse and guitar capture aspects of

Figure 9. Jimmy and his horse lamp in *Thelma & Louise* (1991)

Jimmy's life, revealing his identity as an aging lounge singer still waiting for his lucky break. With his cowboy looks and Elvis persona, Jimmy exudes a certain boyishness and reluctance to grow up, qualities that may have been charming to Louise at one time but now seem to have lost their appeal.

Although he manages to come through for Louise, bringing her the money she requested, Jimmy has a serious flaw, namely an explosive temper. In the motel room, he blows up in anger, knocking over furniture and items on the table when he realizes he is not in control of the situation or Louise, and that she is not going to tell him what is going on. Jimmy fails to take any responsibility for his violent reaction and their troubled relationship, even after he indicates that he wants to commit himself to Louise. Earlier, during a phone call when she asks Jimmy if he loves her, he pauses a bit too long before answering. As both scenes indicate, Jimmy prefers the wild life and remains ambivalent about commitment or emotional attachments.

Hal Slocumb, the detective in charge of the murder investigation, is similarly identified as a Western character in part by surrounding objects, for example a Remington-style horse sculpture that appears in one of his scenes. As the lawman tasked with bringing in the female renegades, Hal tries to empathize with Thelma and Louise and seems to understand their plight. Along with the unnamed African American cyclist they encounter later on their journey, he is one of the only sympathetic male characters in the film. Hal nevertheless answers the call of duty as a sheriff whose job involves bringing in the two outlaws. His phone conversation with Louise in which he keeps her on the line and tells her sympathetically that he knows what happened in Texas becomes the means by which the FBI is able to pinpoint the women's location. Ultimately, both Jimmy and Hal show the limits of male heroism in this Western, as neither character is able to save or rescue Thelma and Louise from the escalating and dire circumstances they face.

The film's critique of gender appears in other aspects of the production design. Numerous scenes feature phallic imagery as a way to showcase the problems of masculinity, male privilege, and sexual double standards. In addition to guns and cars, such imagery includes water hoses, gas nozzles,

Figure 10. Hal and his horse sculpture in *Thelma & Louise* (1991)

telephone poles, cigarettes, the hair dryer J. D. uses as his prop for rob-bing a bank, and the policeman's finger pointing out of the bullet hole that Thelma shoots into the trunk of the patrol car.[13] As Ann Putnam notes, these elements announce the West as a "male landscape," a setting marked by various threats and dangers that the two women will be forced to negotiate "at their own peril." The spaces Thelma and Louise encoun-ter in the film are often "awash in waves of pumping testosterone," she points out, with "spouting steam, spraying planes, spilling hoses, pump-ing oil riggers, and men pumping iron and pumping gas."[14] Such implicit threats also appear in modern forms of transportation that highlight the gendered politics of mobility, whether in the form of imposing semitrucks, honking cars, blasting trains, or buzzing helicopters. These entities are a menacing presence that restrict and impede the women's freedom and movement on the road.

In the Western, industrialization and technology often appear as threats to the region's identity as a place of escape and freedom, with mod-ern forms of transportation frequently representing powerful forces of change. In the settler imagination, railroads often mark the encroachment of the modern world, at times something to be welcomed by the commu-nity and at other times foreshadowing the demise of the West.[15] Trains "led to the establishment of standard time, shortened travel duration, and reduced transportation costs," as Robin L. Murray and Joseph K. Heu-mann point out in their book *Gunfight at the Eco-Corral*. Railroads carried passengers from the American East to the American West and prompted the development of settler towns along the tracks, thus dramatically alter-ing the region's landscape and ecologies.[16] Railroads also brought white women, the harbingers of family, domesticity, and the imagined end of the West. This development is depicted humorously in Stephen Crane's

Figure 11. Spouting water as phallic imagery in *Thelma & Louise* (1991)

Figure 12. Pumping iron in *Thelma & Louise* (1991)

Figure 13. Pumping oil in *Thelma & Louise* (1991)

1898 famous short story, "The Bride Comes to Yellow Sky," which opens with the arrival of a great Pullman train carrying the marshal's new wife to a West Texas town, her appearance symbolizing the ultimate defeat of outlaw Scratchy Wilson. A few years later, novelist Frank Norris's *The Octopus: A Story of California* (1901), also signals the end of the imagined West by means of the railroad in a gruesome sequence that features a herd of sheep meeting their death in the form of an oncoming train.[17] In *Thelma & Louise*, the blasting railroad disrupts the protagonists' mobility and plans for escape. Speeding by them on the tracks, the train interrupts the women's getaway route as they try to move westward. It nearly drowns out their words and adds intensity to the scene in which Louise hints about what happened to her in Texas; the sound of the railroad forces her to yell out that she doesn't want to go through Texas and that she's not going to talk about it anymore with Thelma.

Marita Sturken addresses other forms of modern technology that threaten the women's freedom and mobility. Discussing *Thelma & Louise* as an outlaw movie, Sturken references the FBI's surveillance technologies that track the female bandits to the edge of the Grand Canyon. In the genre of the outlaw film, ambivalence about advanced forms of technology often shapes plot, conflict, and character. "Mechanization is part of what both defines and destroys these outlaws," Sturken points out. "Cassidy and Sundance rob trains, but their world is one of horses and the open range. Bonnie and Clyde are dependent on cars for the getaways and even take on gang member C.W. precisely because he can repair them." In this sense, Sturken notes, the "story of the American outlaw is also a story about encroaching modernity."[18] While the '66 Thunderbird enables the women's escape, Thelma and Louise frequently encounter other menacing vehicles that undercut their freedom, such as the eighteen-wheeler tanker truck with the lewd driver, the patrol cars that hunt them down, the helicopter that looms overhead during their final moments and, earlier in the film, the vehicle in the parking lot of the Silver Bullet where Harlan pins Thelma down and tries to rape her.

Extending Sturken's discussion of technology to the context of the Western specifically, we can understand surveillance equipment as another sign of an encroaching modernity that disrupts the fantasy of Western freedom. Throughout the film, surveillance technologies serve as the long arm of the law, thwarting the women's efforts to escape the scene of the crime.[19] In this way, the phallic telephone poles that appear across the landscape carry additional significance as a means for tracking down the two women. They become a reminder of the imposing presence of the law and of male power, as well as an offshoot of the modern world's technology, which Hal and his team of agents employ in pinpointing the women's location near the end of the movie.

Examining the historical context in which the popular Western emerged, Richard Etulain explains that the genre began during the era of industrialization, a time when a modernizing America faced threats to its identity as a rural and agricultural nation.[20] In the late nineteenth century, historian Frederick Jackson Turner delivered his famous frontier thesis, which depicted western spaces as a crucial American terrain that helped forge the nation's identity as something distinct from Europe. In Turner's lecture, the West was imagined as the site for new beginnings for a white settler population and as a landscape of authenticity whose fate was perennially under threat in the modern era.[21]

*Thelma & Louise* engages these ideas about the West from a gendered perspective. The main characters' old-timey names, for instance, hark back to the late nineteenth or early twentieth century, the period in which Westerns are typically set. But despite their names, the female characters are modern women who try to move beyond the outmoded ideas about gender, sexuality, and domesticity that restrict their lives. The film plays off other popular sentiments about the West, particularly ideas regarding authenticity. As they move westward, the two outlaws start to become more themselves. Their makeup comes off, their hair is set free, and as Khouri suggests, their "inner beauty" becomes more apparent.[22] Addressing the powerful draw of authenticity that shapes popular fantasies of the West, William Handley and Nathaniel Lewis point out there are "few terms at play in the history of this vast region that have as wide a reach and relevance" as authenticity. As they explain, "There is no region in America that is as haunted by the elusive appeal, legitimating power, and nostalgic pull of authenticity."[23]

Yet if the West of *Thelma & Louise* is imagined as a place where the characters can claim their true or authentic selves, the ideal is undermined forcefully at various points in the film. While the West is initially imagined as a site of retreat, the promise of freedom that often propels the genre and its modern offshoot of the road film is continually thwarted. The world map displayed on the wall in the motel where they stay, for instance, becomes an ironic statement about their efforts to evade the law. While the map features a vast terrain and seems to depict an open landscape of possibility, the film continually highlights the difficulties of mobility and the impossibility of escape for the female outlaws. Likewise, the Texaco and 76 gas station signs they encounter when they stop to refuel call forth the restrictions and violence they are trying to avoid: the Texas-owned gas company is a stark reminder of what Louise wants to forget about the Lone Star state, and the 76 sign is a reminder of the independence they don't actually have.

Figure 14. Texaco and 76 signs in *Thelma & Louise* (1991)

Figure 15. Texaco sign as a traumatic reminder of the past in *Thelma & Louise* (1991)

As a road film, *Thelma & Louise* references elements in other movies in the genre, particularly *Easy Rider* (Dennis Hopper, 1969), a film about the counterculture that also explores the limits of American freedom. *Thelma & Louise* engages this theme through images of the US flag, which appear meaningfully in both films. As a way of commenting on popular national beliefs and myths of identity, the 1991 movie frequently showcases the stars and stripes across trucker hats, on storefront windows, and at gas stations in the West, often in an ironic nod to the lack of freedom the female characters experience on their journey. The movie thus gestures toward sentiments also shaping *Easy Rider*, whose protagonists repurpose elements of Americana as a way of critiquing national ideals and beliefs. When Wyatt, the cowboy figure played by Peter Fonda, wears the US flag on his jacket, he makes a powerful statement about the counterculture and its visions of freedom, liberty, and American identity. At the end of the film, however, Wyatt, his friend Billy (Dennis Hopper), and the flag meet a terrible fate when they are drawn into the path of violence. The closing scene shows Wyatt placing his stars-and-stripes jacket across the bloody body of Billy, who is shot down by two men in a pickup truck. Soon afterward, Wyatt too is blown off the road by the same men, his motorcycle exploding in a ball of fire.

If *Easy Rider* positions the counterculture as a means for interrogating American liberty and freedom, then *Thelma & Louise* offers feminism as a way of extending those critiques. The female characters face numerous struggles in their efforts to claim power and control over their bodies and lives. In addition to gender and sexuality, economic realities constrain their experiences. In an early scene, Thelma appears in the domestic realm—she is shown as being financially dependent on her breadwinner husband Darryl, who expresses his class and gender privilege by exerting control over her actions and thoughts. In contrast, Louise is not married and supports herself by working outside the home. Her job as a waitress at a diner, however, is low paying and not likely to offer a means of getting ahead.

At the Silver Bullet, Louise leaves a generous tip for their waitress, Lena (Lucinda Jenney), perhaps signaling the possibilities of forging class and gender solidarity with other working women. Lena also leaves a tip of her own in the form of a sly warning to Thelma and Louise, when she asks Harlan if he's "bothering these poor girls" after he joins their table. "Well, it's a good thing they're not all as friendly as you," she says. Lena rolls her eyes to signal her disdain for him when she brings drinks to the table and tells the women, "This one's on Harlan." In this way, Lena exerts power and agency in her effort to warn the women about a predatory man. These elements appear again in a scene when law officer Hal shows up to investigate the crime. The easy banter between Hal and Lena, including a bit of flirting on her part, inverts the power dynamics often shaping hetero-sexual relationships in the Western, with Lena acting as the initiator. Hal, meanwhile, appears a bit embarrassed and surprised at the sexual atten-tion he receives, caught off guard by her boldness. "Aren't you gonna offer me some teen-eeny, widdy-biddy, little drink?" Lena teases him. "Behave yourself," Hal says with a smile, avoiding eye contact with her.

The moment stands in stark contrast to previous scenes in the film that involve men's sexual privilege and their sense of entitlement. When Louise points a gun at Harlan in the Silver Bullet parking lot, he tries to cover his act, laughing off the attempted rape as "just havin' a little fun." Meanwhile, Darryl illustrates sexual double standards when he cheats on his wife, lies to her about working late, and expects her to stay home and make him dinner. In these instances, both Harlan and Darryl claim privi-leges that do not extend to the women in their lives.

By foregrounding gender, sexuality, and power in these scenes, the movie highlights problems of freedom and identity that often shape Western characters. The ideal figure in the genre is typically a self-possessed and sovereign individual male—a white settler hero or Ameri-can Adam—who is unencumbered by the restrictions of history and the attachments of family or community.[24] These characters frequently devote themselves to ensuring the cause of freedom in ways that exemplify larger national beliefs. "There is no higher value than freedom in American politics and political thought," Elizabeth R. Anker points out in her book *Ugly Freedoms*. "It is the foundational value that the country embodies, that citizens desire, and that the state is said to defend."[25]

In the Western, ideas of freedom and liberty often lend meaning to the action of the film while elevating the spaces of the West and the heroism of the white male hero. Yet the practice of freedom as an "always celebrated virtue" may work to hide systems of domination as well as injuries that are produced by its pursuit.[26] In Westerns, these systems include settler colonialism, racism, male privilege, and environmental destruction, to name just a few. Forms of oppression that often legitimate this "principled" ideal underpin the struggles facing the female characters in *Thelma & Louise*. As Anker explains, "Throughout US history, freedom has taken shape as individual liberty and emancipation from tyranny, but it has also taken shape as the right to exploit and the power to subjugate."[27] Jodi Byrd addresses this problem in her book *The Transit of Empire: Indigenous Critiques of Colonialism*, noting that efforts to ensure freedom in the US nation-state are often established through "force, violence, and genocide in order to make freedom available for some and not others."[28] When Harlan asserts his freedom to engage in what he considers to be a "little fun," Louise enlightens him about how his liberties come at the expense of her friend. "Looks like you have a real fucked up idea of fun," she tells Harlan. "In the future, when a woman's cryin' like that, she isn't havin' any fun."

The freedoms often highlighted in the Western are also undercut by the ending of the film, when the two women commit themselves to each other rather than cut the other loose in the hopes of securing their own safety. Although Louise fires the shot that sets in motion their tremendous calamity and Thelma makes a series of mistakes that place them in even greater trouble, the two friends do not abandon each other. Instead, their shared struggles help the women forge stronger ties and deeper attachments to each other, the opposite of the "ugly freedoms" that Anker describes. As she points out, when "freedom is envisioned as autonomous agency or masculinist heroism, then practicing freedom through dependence and mutual action might seem laughable or humiliating."[29] In the film, this interdependent sense of freedom signals the power of the women's relationship and offers an important shift in the Western genre by centering the promise of female friendship rather than female rivalry.

These moments also shift the film's point of reference. While we might consider how *Thelma & Louise* extends and challenges the plots and conflicts of the Western, something else happens if we look at the movie through a different reference point, namely feminism and the critique of gender privilege. Through this lens, the terrifying scene of sexual assault that takes place in the parking lot of the Silver Bullet and the unspoken memory of what happened to Louise in Texas call to mind similar scenes of sexual threat and assault appearing in earlier women's Westerns.

We might look at the case of *The Wind* (Victor Sjöström, 1928), for instance, a silent film featuring Lillian Gish that was adapted by screenwriter Frances Marion from the novel of the same name written by Dorothy Scarborough. *The Wind* tells the story of a white woman from the East who travels to her cousin's isolated ranch in Texas, where she is driven insane by loneliness, the harsh weather on the plains, memories of a violent settler history, and the intrusion of a predatory cattleman who sexually assaults her.[30] We might also reference *The Belle Starr Story* (1968), a rape-revenge film cowritten and codirected by Piero Cristofani and Lina Wertmüller that features Elsa Martinelli in the main role. The figure of

Belle Starr has appeared in at least nineteen movies and television shows since 1928 and, prior to that, made many appearances in popular dime novels.[31] The 1968 film transforms a male-dominated plot of the Western, where men take on the role of avenging crimes against women, into one featuring a gunslinging female outlaw who seeks justice for survivors of sexual violence.[32]

While shifting the movie's reference points to the women's Western, Khouri also routes her script through another film tradition, drawing on elements of the screwball comedy. Through clever banter between the women and the use of unexpected humor, *Thelma & Louise* extends the tradition even as the film addresses a number of decidedly "unfunny" moments, as Victoria Sturtevant points out.[33] Critic Peter N. Chumo II offers a useful reading of *Thelma & Louise* in the context of the genre, noting the ways it uses classic screwball comedy sequences, such as escaping the constraints of life by taking to the road, acting out different social roles, and discarding an old identity in favor of something new.[34] As a screwball comedy Western, *Thelma & Louise* may be something of a rarity, joining a small group that includes *Calamity Jane* (1953), *Raising Arizona* (1987), and the television show *Northern Exposure* (1990–1995).[35]

While Westerns tend to favor male characters and masculine pursuits in a rural setting, screwball comedies often celebrate sexual equality in urban spaces and feature both strong female and male characters. As William Rothman explains, screwball comedies tend to center on a heterosexual relationship as it unfolds through quick and clever dialogue that reveals the wit and intelligence of both characters. Rothman references the "comedy of remarriage," Stanley Cavell's term for a subset of the screwball comedy, where the meanings and rituals of conventional heterosexual romance are often subverted. Drawing on Cavell's work, Rothman notes that these films frequently pose questions about what constitutes a "relationship worth having" and what it means to be "a full human being."[36] In many of these movies, the couple must overcome obstacles "that are between and within themselves," problems they cannot resolve without first "achieving a radically changed philosophical perspective."[37] Such observations about the screwball comedy go far in explaining what is at stake at the ending of *Thelma & Louise*. At the film's conclusion, the two women can't turn back or turn themselves in precisely because they face impossible social obstacles that make their life as it currently exists unbearable. In that sense, the two characters must move forward and explore possibilities that may exist beyond the abyss.

From the beginning of the film, screwball elements appear in ways that destabilize the Western. In early scenes, for instance, Louise channels the sharp and witty females often featured in 1930s and 1940s Hollywood films. Wearing deep-red lipstick, a flowy scarf tied under her chin, and dark sunglasses as she drives the two of them in her open-top convertible toward their weekend cabin, Louise makes several quick and clever comments that pay tribute to strong female characters in earlier movies. While Rothman argues that the female screwball character may risk losing her equal standing with the male lead because of her odd behavior or thinking, Khouri's script uses a series of role reversals that enable crucial shifts in gender, power, and knowledge.

We see this transformation in the film's treatment of Thelma. Initially, she is positioned as an oddball character who is childlike and not fully mature. Audiences first meet her the morning she leaves for the weekend trip, sneaking bites from a candy bar that she stashes in the freezer, as if desire itself has to be meted out in small, child-size portions. Advertisements cut out from newspapers and magazines appear on her kitchen

Figure 16. Louise as a 1940s Hollywood actress in *Thelma & Louise* (1991)

walls, cabinets, and refrigerator. Numerous remodeling projects in various stages of completion are underway around her home. Such scenes suggest that Thelma is merely playing house rather than living an actual adult life, her relationship with the abusive Darryl a prime cause for much of this stunted growth.

Thelma's position in the domestic sphere is significant in other ways as well. Critic John Lenihan writes about common gender roles in the Western. Although he doesn't specify race, his observations center on the experiences of white settler characters. The Western, he argues, tends to be "male-oriented by virtue of its emphasis on physical, violent conflict," while the "ideal [white] woman" is frequently "portrayed as a domesticating influence on the hero and . . . a symbol of civilization's triumph over wilderness."[38] In this sense, the contrasting gender roles in *Thelma & Louise* are treated somewhat comically, with Darryl often blowing up in anger when his power is even minutely threatened and Thelma barely able to keep her home orderly and clear of chaos.

Initially, Thelma's naïve attitudes position her as the opposite of her more experienced friend Louise. Lenihan argues that the Western in general tends to feature two opposing types of (white) women. The first type includes a "virtuous" domestic female, frequently a schoolteacher, wife, or daughter of a rancher. The second type includes the public female who is experienced and "eroticized," often a "saloon woman" or sex worker.[39] Initially, in Khouri's screwball Western, Thelma serves as the domestic female whose identity is tied to her husband and home. Meanwhile, Louise works in a diner and her worldly experiences allow her to recognize that her younger friend deserves better than Darryl, an opinion she shares with Thelma on more than one occasion. Louise also senses immediately that both Harlan and J. D. are not to be trusted and is likewise wary of Hal, remaining unconvinced that the detective will be able to successfully help them out of the crisis.

Drawing on the screwball comedy tradition, the women's contrasting roles as innocent or experienced eventually shift. The transformation comes after a scene with the con artist J. D., who teaches Thelma how to rob a bank. A common device in Westerns involves men teaching women how to use a weapon, with scenes of gunplay often serving as a thinly veiled metaphor for sexual seduction. After spending a wild night at a motel with J. D., Thelma comes down to breakfast, her messy hair and goofy grin indicating that she's had an evening of pleasurable sex, a first for her. Thelma confesses to Louise, "Now I know what the fuss is all about." The two women celebrate the moment until Louise realizes that the envelope with her life savings is still in the motel room. The two women race upstairs, only to find the money gone and J. D. nowhere to be found. Thelma chastises herself, pacing the room while lamenting how she's never "been lucky, not once in her whole life." Louise, who has been a figure of strength up to this point, breaks down in tears.

After they realize they have very limited means to escape and Louise is overcome with despair, the power dynamics in the screwball Western shift and Thelma suddenly assumes control of the situation. Film critic Molly Haskell, an admitted fan of the screwball comedy, notes how the genre often uses "anarchy" as a means by which the powerless confront the powerful.[40] In the film, Thelma's unpredictable behavior frequently disarms her potential foes or anyone who underestimates her capabilities. Indeed, Thelma proves her talent in matching Louise's outlaw behavior when she holds up a convenience store and later locks a frightened and bawling police office (Jason Beghe) in the trunk of his car. While hand-cuffing the police officer, Thelma tells Louise to shoot the radio in his patrol car. After Louise fires at the dashboard radio playing music, Thelma tells her sternly, "The *police* radio, Louise." Thelma then directs the officer to the trunk of his car as he begs for his life and mentions he has a wife and kids. "You do?" she says to the policeman before ordering him into the trunk at gunpoint. "Well, you're lucky. You be sweet to 'em, especially your wife. My husband wasn't sweet to me and look how I turned out."

Through moments of humor and the various challenging experiences that bind the two women together, it becomes clear that this screwball comedy Western will not be centered on restoring heterosexual relationships. Addressing the function of sexuality and gender in many Westerns, Leslie Fiedler points out that "every genre embodies an archetype, at whose heart is a characteristic myth of love," or what he calls "the erotic center." Fiedler describes this myth as a "transitory and idyllic love between two males in the wilderness, one a white refugee from white civilization, the other a nonwhite member of a group that has been exploited"; it is a myth that calls into being forms of hostility toward white women, "the enforcers of civility and normality."[41] Khouri's script not only disrupts the erotic center of the myth Fiedler addresses by focusing on two white women, but it also queers the screwball comedy plotline in the process. Just before they ride over the cliff, the women kiss and hold hands. In the history of films about lesbian desire, as Cathy Griggers points out, "the kiss is usually how everything starts." She suggests that the women's final act of going over the edge of the Grand Canyon marks the "ecstasy of the abyss."[42]

The reversals often favored by the screwball comedy appear in other scenes as well. Darryl, for instance, becomes an unexpected screwball character when he falls over construction equipment left in the driveway on his way to work, accidentally steps into a box of pizza while talking with Hal, and nearly topples down the stairs at the police station after learning that J. D. has slept with Thelma. Meanwhile, as a runaway wife, Thelma abandons the domestic realm, reversing conventional gender roles by leaving Darryl to take on the household duties. Becoming a housewife of sorts, Darryl serves food to Hal and the FBI officers who have camped out in his living room. Later the reversal becomes apparent again when Darryl admonishes them for making a mess of things, suggesting they should be tidier and more considerate of his home.[43]

These screwball comedy reversals end up referencing another movie genre that is also frequently considered a male-dominated form. In *Thelma & Louise*, the women face numerous risks on their journey that involve fending off rapists and abusers, avoiding near collisions with other vehicles, escaping various crime scenes, fleeing law enforcement, and helping a truck driver (Marco St. John) learn better manners. With these scenes, *Thelma & Louise* nods to the tradition of the action-adventure film. Yet in Khouri's screenplay, when the screwball plot meets the action-adventure movie, a crucial change occurs. This time it involves another gender role reversal, with Hal and the FBI agents portrayed as either glued to the TV while they watch a news show featuring Thelma in the act of committing armed robbery or depicted in a static position as they wait to trace a phone call from the women. The scenes place the men in somewhat passive roles while the two women appear in a series of high-speed and dangerous adventures which culminate in the dramatic, over-the-cliff conclusion.[44]

One could argue that there are actually two endings of the film. The first ending involves the scene with Thelma and Louise driving over the edge of the Grand Canyon. Following this moment, the movie includes a flashback montage featuring key moments in their friendship. Roger Ebert considered the final closing sequence a botched ending, a "vulgar carnival of distraction" that undermined the "payoff" of the scene of the women driving over the edge of the Grand Canyon, which ends in a freeze-frame.[45] This juxtaposition of before and after shots may appear to compromise the unexpected and powerful ending of going over the cliff, yet it may also accomplish something else by prompting viewers to consider the complex and meaningful experiences that have occurred during the women's journey together. Ultimately, these experiences transform the two characters. We see Thelma and Louise move from their location of restriction in their traditionally gendered roles at the beginning of the film to a place where they become fearless partners who defy cultural limitations, sexual double standards, and gendered violence. In this sense, they risk going beyond the edge precisely in order to claim control over their lives and forge new identities, relationships, and Western futures.

# 2. | "A Love Letter to the West"

To argue that *Thelma & Louise* burst onto the cultural scene when it appeared in theaters during the summer of 1991 would not be an exaggeration. Indeed, the movie became an "explosive spectacle," as Sharon Willis explains, a film that "overflowed its frame in the popular press," where it inspired both popular and critical discussion.[1] In some cases, the movie received sharp criticism and was accused of being both anti-male and antifeminist. A common complaint centered on the film's alleged male bashing and its cast of clueless and cartoonish men. In his well-known review originally published by U.S. News and World Report, for instance, John Leo criticizes *Thelma & Louise* for its "fascist" themes, taking issue in particular with its repeated use of "transformative violence," which, in his estimation, made it seem less like a lesson from "[Andrea] Dworkin" than a "Mussolini speech."[2]

During the summer of 1991, *Newsweek* also ran a story titled "Women Who Kill Too Much" that highlighted some of the popular responses to the film. The article cites the surprisingly "virulent criticism" the movie received by some reviewers who condemned its "pathetic stereotypes," "thoughtless, aggressive acts," and "sadistic . . . explosive revenge." *Newsweek* included a reply from screenwriter Callie Khouri, who felt the need to clarify that the film is "not hostile toward men. It's hostile toward idiots."[3]

*Time* magazine weighed in that summer as well, printing a cover that promised to explain "Why Thelma & Louise Strikes a Nerve." The title of Margaret Carlson's feature story asks pointedly, "Is This What Feminism Is All About?" and Carlson argues that the women's movement seems to have "never happened" for the female leads. For Carlson, *Thelma & Louise* fails to provide true freedom or expanded choices for its main female characters and instead holds out a false promise about the "male fantasy" of "life on the road." The reviewer criticizes in particular the sexual agency that Thelma claims, pointing to the scene where she sleeps with the young drifter J. D. Not only did the idea of transcendent and life-changing sex seem to be a cliché to the reviewer, but the moment also required "a breathtaking midair somersault of faith to believe Thelma would be eager to take up with another stranger so soon" after the attempted rape in Arkansas. Such flaws, Carlson argues, leave viewers such as herself wondering if screenwriter Khouri "isn't just fronting for Hugh Hefner."[4]

Over the years, the film's screenwriter and actors have addressed the moral panic generated by the movie. Khouri defended the script by saying that "if you're a man and you felt threatened by it, now you know how women feel every time they walk into the movie theater."[5] Geena Davis also responded to the criticism. "Men who feel threatened by this movie are identifying with the wrong characters," she argued. "It's not a movie to set the record straight. This is a movie about people claiming responsibility for their own lives."[6] Reflecting on her first impression of the script, Susan Sarandon confessed she had not anticipated the strong reactions about screen violence or the backlash that the film would receive. "I saw this as 'Butch Cassidy and the Sundance Kid,'" but featuring "women and trucks . . . kind of a cowboy movie," she explained.[7]

While she was working on the script, Khouri says, she imagined the main female characters as "two average women who were not criminals" and were only outlaws in the sense that the world they live in is "so insane" that they couldn't "help but break the law" in trying to be themselves.[8] In casting the lead roles for the movie, a number of possibilities emerged, with Frances McDormand and Holly Hunter initially considered for the parts. Later, Goldie Hawn and Meryl Streep became contenders. Eventually, Jodie Foster and Michelle Pfeiffer were given the roles but Foster dropped out to take the leading part in *The Silence of the Lambs* (1991), while Pfeiffer took a main role in *Love Field* (1992). Their departure from the film allowed Geena Davis to play the role of the charming but naïve housewife Thelma Dickinson and Susan Sarandon to take the role of the more experienced and somewhat jaded waitress Louise Sawyer.[9]

Meanwhile, Billy Baldwin was first considered for the character of J. D., but dropped out of the running after accepting a part in Ron Howard's *Backdraft* (1991).[10] Brad Pitt, a relatively unknown actor at the time, was eventually cast as the young cowboy J. D.—a name referencing James Dean or perhaps "juvenile delinquent," depending on which critic you ask.[11] The film provided the actor with a breakout role that helped launch his path to Hollywood stardom. As Edmond Y. Chang aptly put it, Brad Pitt's performance in *Thelma & Louise* "forever enshrined" J. D. as a "shirtless scalawag" figure, a "sensitive but bad boy 'outlaw'" who was "a little dangerous and a whole lot titillating" with his "hairdryer, cowboy hat, tawny torso and twang."[12]

Initially, Khouri considered directing the movie herself as a low-budget indie film. Working in Los Angeles as a line producer for music videos, she contacted her friend and colleague Amanda Temple about helping her secure financing for the film. Temple eventually gave the script to Mimi Polk Gitlin, who ran director Ridley Scott's production company,

Figure 17. J. D. poses as an outlaw in *Thelma & Louise* (1991)

Percy Main Productions. Scott wanted to produce the film and, having trouble finding someone who wasn't interested in altering the story, soon realized he wanted to direct it himself.[13] Critic Amy Taubin argues that at first glance, *Thelma & Louise* may seem to be a departure for Scott, as a film "driven by character rather than events," but she then goes on to point out how the movie shares similarities with other films the director had made. Like *Alien* (1979) or *Blade Runner* (1982), *Thelma & Louise* offers "an allegorical narrative within a realistically detailed visual world."[14] Yet at least one reviewer took issue with what he saw as the director's overreliance on "'Alien'-size hardware." In his review for the *Seattle Times*, Michael Upchurch argues that the director went overboard with scenes featuring "gratuitous pyrotechnics," especially the explosion of the semitruck, which appears "to have been included for sheer spectacle" rather than for what it might "add to the movie."[15]

For many audiences, *Thelma & Louise* resonated differently, less as an action-adventure movie than a film that called to mind previous Westerns about outlaws on the run, such as *Butch Cassidy and the Sundance Kid*

(1969) or *The Wild Bunch* (1969).[16] Viewers who recognized *Thelma & Louise* as a Western were often especially delighted by its feminist critique and the way it pushed back against some of the genre's more limited views of power and sexuality. "The draw of the film," Rita Felski explains, has much to do with how it confronted the "impoverished plotlines" of movie history and offered "a corrective to a restrictive repertoire of roles for women." In this way, the movie contributed to "a sharpening public realization of how severely gender norms had constrained possibilities of character and plot."[17] Khouri put it well herself when she remarked about her own frustrations with the passive roles that female characters are often assigned in movies. "They were never driving the story," she noted, "because they were never driving the car."[18]

Some viewers, like critic Marjorie Baumgarten, were pleased by Khouri's efforts to place women in the driver's seat. In her review for the *Austin Chronicle*, Baumgarten describes *Thelma & Louise* as a "female *Butch Cassidy and the Sundance Kid*" with the female characters facing new conflicts in a familiar setting. For her, *Thelma & Louise* departs from the earlier Western by offering a different ending for its female characters, not a shootout in a blaze of gunfire but something more ambiguous and perhaps more meaningful. After Louise fires the fateful shot at Harlan in the parking lot of the Silver Bullet, the two women embark on a journey westward that leads them "to the end of the road," which mythically is situated "somewhere in the heart of John Ford country," she explains. A feminist film "without ever becoming didactic or polemic," the movie shows that breaking out of gender confinements and narrow life choices may send the two friends on a "road less traveled" but eventually allows them to claim better "dreams."[19]

*New York Times* critic Janet Maslin likewise applauded the movie, recognizing *Thelma & Louise* as an important contribution to the development of various film genres. Praising Khouri's "sparkling screenplay," her review notes that the film showcases director Scott's "previous untapped talent" for "exuberant comedy" and his ability to capture a "vibrant American imagery, notwithstanding his English roots." Observing that *Thelma & Louise* "reimagines the buddy film" with "freshness and vigor," Maslin argues that the movie doesn't offer "moral justification for Louise's violent act" but instead manages to make "this and other outlaw gestures" in its story "at least as understandable as they would be in a traditional western."[20]

In her essay on the film, Manohla Dargis describes *Thelma & Louise* as a road movie that recasts the tradition, "custom-fitting it to female specifications" by locating its story "in the politics of the body."[21] Connecting *Thelma & Louise* to previous outlaw couple movies such as *Bonnie and Clyde* (Arthur Penn, 1967) and *Badlands* (Terrence Malick, 1973), Dargis argues that the film extends the tradition by featuring conflicts about gender and sexuality as crucial elements in its story line. In *Thelma & Louise*, the lead characters "become outlaws the moment they seize control of their bodies," their renegade identities "forced on them by a gendered lack of freedom," such that their real crimes are not murder but "subjectivity."[22] Dargis notes that in a particularly crucial scene featuring "red buttes and mesas" commonly associated with the "most memorable Westerns," the camera opens to a panoramic shot of the land and then moves back to a close-up of the female leads. For her, the sequence foregrounds the deep connections the two friends have forged with each other while allowing viewers to recognize their status as both "domesticated and uncivilized."[23] To Dargis, the film insists that "the female body is not a landscape to be mapped, a frontier under conquest." Instead, the movie offers a powerful story that addresses the characters' contradictory desires for "liberation" and "empathetic connection."[24]

For some viewers, though, *Thelma & Louise* seemed to thwart this reading, its unexpected over-the-cliff ending upsetting possibilities for feminist agency, freedom, or even the characters' own futures. Critic Amy Taubin felt betrayed by the final scene and in an interview suggested an ending that has its own problems. Considering that a handful of "open-ended outlaw films already exist," she wondered why the two characters couldn't be "allowed to live out their days in Mexico" drinking margaritas.[25] Both the screenwriter and director insisted to studio heads that the over-the-cliff sequence remain as it was initially written, and Khouri has stated that the final cut was very close to her original vision for the film.[26] As the law closes in on them, the two women—now considered dangerous criminals—kiss and then hold hands in solidarity, vowing to press forward rather than be caught. As the '66 Thunderbird flies over the edge of the Grand Canyon, the sequence ends in a freeze-frame, placing the female renegades above the abyss in a meaningfully ambivalent ending. Khouri has explained that while she indeed "sent them off a cliff," the scene in her mind was not meant to be a suicide or signal the characters' death. "To me, it was allegory. It was flying off into the mass consciousness and leaving them hanging in the air, so that years later, we're still talking about it."[27]

In an interview, the screenwriter mentioned she discussed with director Ridley Scott at length the look she was trying to achieve. "It's got to be a love letter to the West," Khouri insisted. "It should start out looking like a Sears catalogue and end up looking like if Maxfield Parrish painted the West. It should be almost a heavenlike picture."[28] Analyzing recent feminist Westerns in film and television, Krista Comer notes two common trends shaping these stories. One approach relies on revisionism, offering narratives of empowerment in ways that may also implicate white women's experiences in settler history. The other trend presents contemporary stories about white women "at a remove from western frontier histories" who struggle to reckon with the legacies of western history and their own privilege.[29] *Thelma & Louise* is set in the modern world but in some ways is in keeping with certain romanticized views of the West that often shape the genre. The characters' journey to selfhood, for instance, relies on a fantasized idea of the region as a space of promise and possibility. Likewise, while viewers and critics frequently celebrate the film's examination of sexism and misogyny, its revisionist efforts are undercut at times by its failure to acknowledge the story's ties to settler history.

The director's visions of the West reveal some of these limitations. At an early point during filming, Ridley Scott came to believe that the "third major character" in the movie was "the physical landscape" itself.[30] In an interview, he discussed his interest in emphasizing the "exotic" elements he associated with the vast scale of the American West. Such elements have long inspired European filmmakers who were attracted to the Western for these reasons, including Fritz Lang, Sergio Leone, Robert Siodmak, Jacques Tourneur, and Fred Zinnemann, to name just a few.[31] "It's spectacular the way it looks," Susan Sarandon told reporters in 2016 at the ceremony for the film's induction into the National Film Registry. She went on to credit the director for ensuring that the movie expressed an epic, larger-than-life quality. "It could have been a little story and we might not have seemed so heroic, and we might not have earned that liberation at the end, if it had been filmed as a tiny movie," Sarandon explained. "But he put it against John Wayne's backdrop. I'll always be grateful for that."[32]

Alongside these instances, fantasy and nostalgia about the West shape the film in other ways as well. On location hunts for *Thelma & Louise*, for instance, Scott searched for what he considered the "vanishing face of America," a western landscape that was more "Route 66" than "malls and concrete strips," he explained.[33] "Route 66, that piece of heartland, is a little bit of what we Europeans like to think of as the American dream. We've all seen it in movies." Recognizing that Route 66 itself seemed "to be vanishing fast," the director considered centering the movie on that loss by filming landscapes where everything looks "exactly the same every mile of the way." After realizing it would be too depressing to make that particular movie, Scott decided to film the story as a "mythical 'last journey' . . . more like the 'idea' of Route 66." In the end, he sought to feature a "landscape at its most beautiful and expansive."[34]

Settler fears about the loss or decline of the region, along with anxieties about the passage of time, frequently shape the story unfolding in Westerns. At one point during preproduction, Scott chose the telegraph pole as a symbol of the disappearing West. Europeans often "eulogize roads with telegraph poles, and Americans think we're crazy," he explained. Scott searched for days to find such places, but eventually discovered that telegraph poles also seemed to have vanished from the places he visited. The director finally encountered them on a trip to Bakersfield, California, which became a central location in the movie.[35] In an interview, Scott explained that the houses originally set in Arkansas also ended up being filmed elsewhere, in this case at a location near the Warner Brothers lot in Los Angeles, a decision that allowed him and his crew to return home at night after a long day of shooting. The director relocated the filming of other scenes as well when he figured out it wasn't necessary to take nearly 150 crew members to Arizona for only three or four minutes of shooting. And after he realized he couldn't tell the difference between these locations and the settings in the script, he

Figure 18. The western landscape of *Thelma & Louise* (1991)

decided to film the Arizona scenes in Utah at Arches National Park and Canyonlands National Park.[36]

Describing his vision for the film, Scott explained that he found inspiration in the stark landscapes featured in Malick's *Badlands*, an outlaw-couple-on-the run movie also set in the modern West. For scenes featuring interior spaces, Scott drew on the work of American realist painter John Register, who often depicted scenes set in midcentury hotels, with their distinctive diners featuring Formica-topped tables. Inspired by modernist Edward Hopper, Register extended the artist's vision in his own work, creating paintings that often feature a built environment whose atmosphere conveys a sense of alienation and isolation. These scenes seem to lack a human presence, or depict spaces where humans appear disconnected from their environments.[37] This influence may be noted in some of the motel and diner sequences in *Thelma & Louise*: the scenes feature relationships that are coming to an end or that are fractured by deceit and deception, which contrast with the moments of connection and honesty that the two friends experience as they traverse the western landscape.

Figure 19. Escaping the law in *Badlands* (1973)

Figure 20. The modern West of *Badlands* (1973) as inspiration for director Ridley Scott

In discussing her vision for the movie, Khouri also addressed a film that inspired her—another Western, *Lonely Are the Brave* (David Miller, 1962)—for its "beautiful scenery" and modern story line about an alienating and changing America. Based on the 1956 novel *The Brave Cowboy* by Edward Abbey, and with a script by the formerly blacklisted Hollywood writer Dalton Trumbo, the film stars Kirk Douglas as Jack Burns, a modern cowboy confronting a diminished West who ends up on the wrong side of the law and spends much of the film pursued by Sheriff Morey Johnson (played by Walter Matthau). In the opening scene, Jack Burns wakes up to the noise of three airplanes flying overhead as they leave jet streams behind them. Hoping to escape with his horse named Whiskey, the modern cowboy has to first trick the animal into his saddle before he is able to move on. The journey requires a precarious trip across a busy highway with honking trucks and speeding cars swerving by to avoid colliding with Jack and his horse. He eventually arrives at a junkyard filled with old cars, a scene that captures the film's theme about change and loss, the contrast between the fantasy of the Old West and its freedoms and the encroaching New West, which is marked by restrictions and modern transformation.[38] Like Thelma and Louise, Jack encounters a number of challenging situations that snowball into a larger crisis with law enforcement. Like the women, his status on the margins of society and his efforts to survive in a world that offers no place for him help generate audience sympathy.

In interviews, Khouri has spoken about the limitations of gender and the lack of choices for her leading characters as another inspiration for her Western, particularly her realization that the world the two women inhabit often asks them to be "less than" they are.[39] The lack of women's stories on screen became an impetus for Khouri in developing a narrative centered on Thelma and Louise's experiences. "It really irritates me when they say, 'Well, there are only twelve stories.' No, there aren't," she insisted. "There are millions. Even if they have things in common, they're all a little bit different. It's not the same old story. It's our job as writers to make sure they're different."[40]

It's important to recognize that before *Thelma & Louise* arrived in theaters, a number of female outlaws and gunslingers had already appeared in what have been informally classified as "women's Westerns," or films that feature strong female characters and the challenges they face in the West. Some of the more well-known examples include Barbara Stanwyck in *Annie Oakley* (1935), Mae West in *Klondike Annie* (1936), Marlene Dietrich in *Destry Rides Again* (1939) and *Rancho Notorious* (1952), Joan Crawford in *Johnny Guitar* (1954), Jane Fonda in *Cat Ballou* (1965), and Raquel Welch in *Hannie Caulder* (1971).

Stanwyck and Jane Russell appeared in other Westerns too, whether or not they would be classified as women's Westerns. In addition to *Annie Oakley*, Stanwyck appeared in Western films including *Union Pacific* (1939), *The Furies* (1950), *Cattle Queen of Montana* (1954), and *Forty Guns* (1957). She also starred in Western television shows such as *The Big Valley* (1965–1969) and had guest appearances on *Wagon Train* (1961–1964). Jane Russell appeared in *The Outlaw* (1943), *The Paleface* (1948), *Montana Belle* (1952), *The Tall Men* (1955), *Johnny Reno* (1966), and *Waco* (1966).

While the category of the woman's Western doesn't typically show up in indexes of film histories, it is possible to locate significant precursors to *Thelma & Louise* that feature compelling female characters in stories set in the West. By recognizing these earlier examples, we can better understand the contexts that set the stage for *Thelma & Louise*. Although much of the hype about the film had to do with the way the movie seemed to burst forth out of nowhere in 1991, it's crucial to point out that Khouri was part of a long history of women filmmakers who sought to tell different stories about gender and the Western. If we look to the historical development of the genre, we may note that female artists were there from the start and their involvement was not insignificant. Cari Beauchamp points out, for instance, that copyright records from the early years of cinema indicate that almost half of all films made before 1925 were written by women.[41] They likewise wrote, directed, produced, and starred in Western movies beginning in the silent era, when the genre was just starting to be consolidated. No doubt these filmmakers also sought to tell different stories on screen just as Khouri did, yet because the Western came to be regarded as a male genre and because women's stories may not regularly fit standard expectations about Western plots, character, and conflicts, women's contributions to the genre have often been overlooked.

Problems of exclusion also appear in literary history, a tradition that influenced the development of cinematic Westerns. In her essay "The Nervous Origins of the Western," Barbara Will argues that gender stereotypes and ideas about modern anxiety disorders were contributing factors in the development of popular Western stories during the late nineteenth century. At a time when many white American women were assigned the "rest cure" as a way of treating anxiety disorders—what was regarded as a widespread affliction among middle- and upper-class white women on the East Coast—their male counterparts were often prescribed the "West cure." The assumptions underpinning men's treatment for nervous disorders positioned the American West as a site for renewing white male selfhood. In this period, stories that featured the heroic adventures of white male characters facing a challenging landscape in the West gained popularity in ways that often excluded the presence of others.[42]

Although the popular Western has often been classified as a male genre, Victoria Lamont argues that it was in fact "founded as much by women writers as by men."[43] She notes that from the beginning of the genre, women writers often recognized the Western's "wide-ranging potential" for diverse stories.[44] In her book *Westerns: A Women's History*, Lamont recovers these efforts. She points to Ann S. Stephens's 1839 *Malaeska*, a popular, successful book that launched the company Beadle and Adams into dime novels in 1860.[45] Lamont also notes that the first cowboy novel beyond the dime novel tradition, *The Administratix* (1889), was written by Colorado author and suffragist Emma Ghent Curtis, and appeared well before the 1902 publication of Owen Wister's *The Virginian*. As the first of its kind, Curtis's Western is also notable for including critiques of gender inequality "long believed" to be a "recent addition to the genre."[46]

Lamont likewise explains that *The Rustler* by Montana writer Frances McElrath appeared the same year as Wister's novel and also took up the Johnson County War as its subject. In addition, she points to *Cogewea, the Half Blood* (1927), an Indigenous Western written by Mourning Dove (Salish) that creates space for Native American characters beyond the narrow confines of the popular Western while offering a critical take on the genre as an instance of colonial discourse.[47] Kirby Brown makes a similar argument, locating Mourning Dove's novel in the tradition of what he calls "Indian Country" Westerns, stories that were centered on Indigenous lives and that "leveraged the familiarity of the genre to upend its decidedly anti-Indian conventions."[48]

Although they were active at every stage of the Western's development, as Lamont points out, women writers were often excluded from literary history, their work classified as sentimental or domestic fiction and thus often not recognized as Westerns.[49] Jane Tompkins makes this argument in her book *West of Everything: The Inner Life of Westerns*. Understanding the popular Western as a male-centered form, she argues that the genre stages a "literary gender war" against the female-authored domestic novel. In doing so, the Western became a tradition "adamantly opposed to anything female."[50] Tompkins notes that Westerns introduce "the viewpoint of women" only for that perspective "to be swept aside, crushed or dramatically invalidated."[51] In this respect, the popular Western "answers the domestic novel," she contends. "It is the antithesis of the cult of domesticity that dominated American Victorian culture. The Western hero, who seems to ride in out of nowhere, in fact comes riding in out of the nineteenth century," and the story often associated with him works to "marginalize and suppress the figure who stood for those ideals."[52]

A problem emerges, however, when scholars overstate their case and disregard the contributions women writers made to the genre. "What began as a systematic omission eventually morphed into explicit denial of the possibility" that women could and did write popular Westerns, Lamont argues.[53] Christine Bold addresses this point as well, connecting these oversights to a larger history of exclusion in the genre. In *The Frontier Club: Popular Westerns and Cultural Power, 1880–1924*, Bold examines how Western fiction became a central form developed and employed by an elite network of eastern white men who sought to consolidate their power by influencing conservation and hunting laws, open-range ranching, immigration policies, Jim Crow rules, and American Indian policies.[54] In actively reshaping "public opinion and federal policy in the key areas of land control, race politics, and emerging mass culture," members of what she calls "the frontier club" produced narratives about the region that "clinched the formula which has long served as the most popular face of America."[55]

By attending to the "cultural baggage carried by the genre," Bold emphasizes how deeply the development of the popular Western depended on the very people that "the frontier club sought to exclude: women, African Americans, 'new' immigrants, and Indigenous peoples."[56] Her analysis acknowledges the importance and significance of a wider group of Americans who were edged out of the Western, noting that while the "power play" she associates with the frontier club took place in print, the presence and cultural influence of this marginalized group are "still legible on the formula."[57] Because Western fiction has frequently served as the source material for Western movies, this literary history becomes an important reference point for understanding the development of the film genre.

Scholars observe, for instance, that as the movie industry became more established, women writers often found themselves edged out when men began realizing that moviemaking could be a lucrative business. In response, women writers sometimes moved from the film industry to the world of literature; many of them found that the publishing industry offered more opportunities for them and typically placed fewer restrictions on the types of stories they wanted to tell. In other words, these women didn't stop writing but instead sought out a different industry where they could exert more control over their stories and careers.[58]

While they faced a number of challenges, women in the film industry nevertheless wrote, directed, produced, and performed in a significant number of Westerns, starting in the early years of cinema when female writers and directors were making headway in the industry. This was at a time when the genre was just developing and trade papers used "Western" (and the like) as a loose descriptor, as in "Wild West drama," "Western comedy," "Indian and western," or "cowboy and Indian" pictures.[59] French-born filmmaker Alice Guy Blaché was one of the more well-known women who wrote and directed early Westerns, including *Parson Sue* (1912), thought to be the first Western directed by a woman.[60] Film historian Alison McMahan argues that from 1896 to 1906, Blaché likewise earned the distinction of being the only woman in the world who was writing and directing movies at the time.[61]

Long before Callie Khouri wrote her screenplay for *Thelma & Louise*, Frances Marion was another prolific and successful woman screenwriter. Between 1915 to 1935, she earned the highest salary as a screenwriter of anyone in the industry, male or female.[62] Marion went on to win two Academy Awards for screenwriting in 1930 and 1932, and also wrote adaptations and scenarios for a number of films, including the gothic Western *The Wind* (Victor Sjöström, 1928).[63] Marion was the only female scriptwriter working without a male writing partner to win an Oscar—until Khouri received the award for *Thelma & Louise* over sixty years later.[64]

Grace Cunard was also a prolific early twentieth-century screenwriter, who not only wrote numerous screenplays, stories, and scenarios for many Westerns but also performed in more than a hundred silent films. Cunard was known for writing roles that called for dangerous stunt work; the plots she developed in these Westerns frequently led to physical injuries for actors, which often delayed production.[65] Ruth Ann Baldwin was also a notable figure in the early years of cinema. She started out as a scenario writer and film editor, and later went on to direct *'49–'17* (1917), a Western parody starring her husband, Leo O. Pierson. The film features a male protagonist tasked with the job of re-creating a western town for his boss, who wants to recapture his glory days during the gold rush era—hence the title *'49–'17*.[66]

Canadian writer, actor, and producer Nell Shipman likewise wrote, directed, and/or starred in Westerns in the early years of cinema, including

*Back to God's Country* (1919), *Something New* (1920), and *Grub Stake* (1923). One of the more widely recognized women who made Westerns in this period, Shipman is known for her plot-reversing stories whose heroines took on the role of the rescuer instead of the victim.[67]

Because movies from the early era are often not as familiar or accessible to today's audiences, viewers may be unaware of these diverse contributions to the Western. In *Women Filmmakers in Early Hollywood*, Karen Ward Mahar points out that women were working in most areas of the US film industry by 1909, with the height of their involvement occurring between 1918 and 1922. By the mid-1920s, however, women who previously had success in the industry were often cast aside as filmmakers, and it was only in the areas of screenwriting and acting that they maintained a significant presence during this period.[68] Lizzie Francke notes in *Script Girls: Women Screenwriters in Hollywood* that Westerns, and particularly B Westerns, provided women writers with the opportunity to continue working in Hollywood. When film studios such as Republic Pictures began double-billing movies at the theater, demand increased for shorter and less expensive features. Francke explains that a handful of female authors, including Adele Buffington, Elizabeth Beecher, Betty Burbridge, and Olive Cooper, were able to continue writing screenplays into the 1930s and 1940s.[69] In the realm of directing and producing, it was not until the late 1970s that the number of women would notably increase.[70]

Although fewer in number than in the thirties and forties, women were also involved in making Westerns during the tail end of the genre's golden era. In the 1950s and 1960s, Ida Lupino, known for her roles in various noir films, directed several episodes for television Westerns, including *Hotel de Paree* (1959–1960), *Have Gun—Will Travel* (1959–1961), *The Rifleman* (1961), *The Virginian* (1966), and *Daniel Boone* (1967). In addition, Leah Brackett is credited as a cowriter on *Rio Bravo* (1959) and as the screenwriter for *El Dorado* (1966), while Carole Eastman wrote the screenplay for *The Shooting* (1966). A decade later, Sonia Chernus was credited as a cowriter for *The Outlaw Josey Wales* (1976).[71]

In *Women in the Western*, Sue Matheson points out that in the post–World War II period, the Western was one of the first American film genres to engage the topic of rape culture. The subject is powerfully addressed in the only spaghetti Western with a woman credited as one of the writers, *The Belle Starr Story* (1968).[72] Jumping ahead to 1990, Ruthanne Lum McCunn's novel *Thousand Pieces of Gold* was made into a movie with a script adapted by writer and filmmaker Anne Makepeace. Directed by Nancy Kelly, the Western tells the story of a Chinese woman who escapes being sold into marriage and sexual servitude by her father and finds her way to a gold camp in the West. She endures anti-Chinese prejudice and sexual assault but eventually makes a life for herself near a mining community in Idaho.

Native American writers, directors, and actors were also important figures in the Western's development. In the early years of the industry, Indigenous performers from Wild West shows were often hired to appear in movies being filmed during the shows' off-season. Eventually these productions helped shift the conventions in movies, with violence between settlers and Indians becoming a popular plotline and basis for the Western.[73] Native American screenwriters were also active in the creation of Westerns and likewise managed to reroute the plots, thus shifting the type of narratives that were being filmed from a settler point of view. Scholars have recounted stories that were told about Indigenous performers who did not adhere to the scripted plots. In some cases, they rewrote the stories by not dying onscreen when they were shot, using live ammunition instead of blanks, and performing ceremonies incorrectly during filming in order to signal their resistance to the parts they were assigned and their interest in reimagining their roles as cinematic performers.[74]

Ho-Chunk actor Lilian St. Cyr, whose stage name was Princess Red Wing, and her husband, James Young Deer, a Nanticoke filmmaker who later identified as Ho-Chunk, were one of Hollywood's original "power couples." Young Deer directed over sixty Indian and Western pictures, and Red Wing was described as "North America's first female silent movie star." The couple eventually went on to claim considerable influence in the film world by making movies that worked against the industry's prevailing racial stereotypes about Native Americans.[75] From 1910 to 1912, films centered on Indians were especially popular—with some studios producing up to fifteen such movies per month.[76] Yet during this time, Indigenous performers and filmmakers often faced significant restrictions. From the late nineteenth century to the first decades of the twentieth century, Native Americans who sought employment off the reservation typically needed to have government permission to travel. Indigenous films themselves were often subject to censorship because they did not feature Indians as eagerly assimilating to white culture but rather "reanimated Native American history as vibrant, viable, and in dialogue with the present and future" in ways that were thought to be dangerous, as critic Michelle Raheja explains.[77]

By 1912, Westerns began to decline, along with short one- and two-reel films, as production companies turned their attention to other subjects. This meant that it would be several decades before Indigenous filmmakers would again reach the level of participation that they experienced in the early years of the movie industry.[78] Recently, Indigenous women have made important inroads as filmmakers and especially as screenwriters. In

1995, the organization Native Women in Film & Television in All Media (NWIFTV) was founded. It would eventually have its own screenings at the annual Red Nation International Film Festival, which takes place just before the Academy Awards each year in order to keep these films on the industry's radar. In 2003, NWIFTV developed its own film festival and is currently the only such festival dedicated to Native and Indigenous women filmmakers. The organization also founded the Native Women Write Screenwriters Lab in 2010. As the #MeToo movement reached national popularity in 2017 and 2018, Joanelle Romero, the founder of #NWIFTV, likewise started the Why We Wear RED initiative, which aims to bring greater awareness to Murdered and Missing Indigenous Women and Girls (MMIWG), a coalition dedicated to ending such acts against Native American women and girls.[79] These contexts provide a more complex picture of the diverse groups involved in making films about the West, their efforts to expand the kind of stories appearing onscreen, and the larger contexts for understanding *Thelma & Louise* as a revisionist Western.

While more than three decades have passed since the movie appeared in theaters, *Thelma & Louise* continues to be an important film that speaks to audiences today, especially in an era when #MeToo and other related conversations have brought increased scrutiny to Hollywood for its toxic masculinity and failures to achieve gender equity and inclusion. Over the years, as new social movements have emerged, additional concerns continue to shape our understanding of Westerns. At a time when Black Lives Matter carries on the fight against racism and structural inequality and when Indigenous movements for sovereignty and decolonization are gaining increased power, the film's relationship to questions of race, particularly whiteness, along with its connections to settler colonial history, require further scrutiny. Likewise, as the fields of ecomedia studies and the environmental humanities gain a greater foothold in the academy and popular culture, it becomes crucial to examine *Thelma & Louise* as a Western and a road film that both critiques and participates in forms of ecological destruction by featuring a high-carbon journey across the West as a means for claiming possibilities and freedom for its protagonists. These are all topics I turn to in greater detail in the following chapter.

# 3. | "We're Fugitives Now"

*Women, Guns, and Violence*

S cholars of the Western have long debated the problem of screen violence, recognizing how conflict and use of force are often central to the unfolding of action and plot as well as the development of character and theme. Addressing the function of violence in the Western, critic Richard Slotkin argues that the use of force is a "normative" element in the genre, "the crisis towards which the energy of the story is directed."[1] Westerns that involve settler fantasies of progress and nation building, for instance, require the conquest of nature and the defeat of racial Others. Often highly stylized and choreographed in the Western, violence is used to uphold settler world views and vindicates a way of being, according to Slotkin.[2]

Lee Clark Mitchell points out that violence in the Western also plays a crucial role in "making the man." In both fiction and film, Westerns often center the white male body in scenes that excessively "punish men as a pretext to allow them to recover, restoring them once more to manhood."[3] Violence likewise elevates certain characters over others in the genre. John Cawelti notes a pattern in the Western that positions "the hero's violence as legitimate and good," while the violence of the enemy is depicted as an "uncontrollable impulse," an unruly force that must be eliminated in order to secure social order by the end of the film.[4]

Although violence is an important feature in the genre, when it comes to depictions of women's use of force in the Western, things often take a different turn. In many cases, gender and sexuality complicate the treatment of violence by highlighting women's power and agency as potential disruptions to the larger social order. In films where female characters use force, violence is frequently unexpected or extraordinary, an element to be passed off, played for laughs, or somehow contained or neutralized. In these instances, violence serves as a challenge to social relations and the status quo, a disruption that needs to be resolved so that gender norms and power dynamics may be restored.

Upon its release, *Thelma & Louise* sparked controversy and debate about its treatment of gender, guns, and violence. Yet as screenwriter Callie Khouri argued, if placed alongside other blockbuster movies that appeared the same year such as *Terminator 2: Judgment Day* (James Cameron, 1991), *Thelma & Louise* may be regarded as showing a certain amount of restraint. Khouri defended the film, noting that "if you put violence in a male context it's unremarkable."[5] She also pointed out that the $17.5 million budget for the film was minimal compared to director Ridley Scott's previous movies. "If it had been guys rather than women, they would have blown up a few more trucks and that would have bumped up the budget."[6]

The violent acts committed by the two women over the course of four or five days include the murder of an attempted rapist, an armed robbery, the kidnapping of a police officer, and the explosion of a semitruck. While taking a man's life, making bodily threats to others, and blowing up property are no small offenses, the controversy surrounding the movie suggests that people were reacting to something more than the transgressions themselves. Some of these responses may have had less to do with the spectacle of violence than with the discomfort of watching men being held accountable for their actions or seeing women asserting agency in their lives. Critic Aspasia Kotsopoulos aptly describes the feelings many female viewers experienced in finally witnessing "a man punished by a woman for his sexism rather than a woman for her sexuality."[7] As noted earlier, some reactions to the film rose to the level of a moral panic that revealed the stakes involved when women claim autonomy and fight back against the sexual and political forces threatening them.

Addressing her unease with how the movie industry often depicts screen violence, Khouri has spoken about her interest in making films that critically examine the moral dimensions of violence. With her screenplay, she tried to avoid trivializing such actions or offering easy resolutions for the main characters and instead wanted to show the consequences and aftermath of using deadly force. Khouri has explained that Thelma and Louise do not set out to become outlaws, but the situations they continually face require them to make difficult and life-changing decisions.[8] The script itself treats the murder of Harlan as an act of revenge rather than an act of self-defense. While it's clear that Harlan had committed a crime in the parking lot of the Silver Bullet and should be held accountable for attempted rape, at the time of the shooting Thelma had broken away from him and the women were already leaving the scene. After the deadly confrontation, Louise herself realizes she has just, as Khouri described, "made the biggest mistake of her entire life" and that her actions have placed her and her friend in grave danger.[9] Grappling with the magnitude of the situation, Louise confesses to Thelma, "I think I got us in a situation where we both could get killed."

In an interview about the film, Khouri explained that Louise's violence at the Silver Bullet is "completely, in every way, out of character for her."[10] When Harlan insults her in the parking lot, thinking he won't be held accountable for his actions, something shifts in Louise and she fires the gun in a rage. The moment is shaped by the built-up frustrations the women have experienced their whole lives in the form of sexual assault, humiliation, betrayal, and degrading male behavior. The film encourages viewers to reflect on the meaning and morality of these actions while also revealing the contexts and circumstances that might push ordinary women to commit violence. In this way, *Thelma & Louise* treats the use of force as a direct outcome of gender inequality and male entitlement, with violence appearing as a response to rape, sexual assault, and ongoing harassment.

Throughout the history of the Western, sexual violence appears with some frequency. As critic Jim Kitses points out, some directors, including John Ford, Sam Peckinpah, and Clint Eastwood, have been criticized for their overreliance on scenes of rape and sexual assault in their films.[11] With its ties to the Indian captivity narrative, the Western often treats the rape or sexual assault of white women allegorically as a means for addressing larger threats to their community.[12] Within the logic of settler colonialism, western landscapes frequently appear as gendered spaces that must be protected from violation by racial Others. Pam Cook argues that a "race/sex/nation conflict" underpins an obsession with miscegenation in the Western and gives rise to "the myth of the rapacious Indian." The sexual double standard, however, means that there is a greater anxiety about white women's relationships with Indigenous men than white men's relationships with Indigenous women.[13] Likewise, there is a racial double standard in the Western regarding fears about the sexual threat of Indigenous

Figure 21. Louise holds a gun to Harlan's head in *Thelma & Louise* (1991)

men rather than the sexual threat of white settler men and a racial double standard involving the women who are assaulted or raped. In *The Outlaw Josey Wales* (Clint Eastwood, 1976), for instance, the rape of an Indigenous woman does not register much outrage in the story, whereas the rape of a white woman is treated as a horrific event, with ominous music and editing marking it as a brutal scene of violence.[14]

In Westerns such as *Stagecoach* (1939), *War Arrow* (1953), *The Missing* (2003), and "The Gal Who Got Rattled" segment of *The Ballad of Buster Scruggs* (2018), rape or the specter of sexual violence against white women is depicted either as a threat to settler society, a violation that western patriarchs must avenge in order to restore the social order, or a form of horror that must be avoided even to the point of death.[15] Sexual violence is also portrayed as a war crime or an act of terror perpetrated against enemies or racial Others in Western films, including *Soldier Blue* (1970), *The Revenant* (2015), and *Wind River* (2017). Rape and anxieties about miscegenation also serve as a threat to white male honor, as depicted in Westerns such as *The Searchers* (1956), *Trooper Hook* (1957), and *For a*

*Few Dollars More* (1965).[16] Michael Madsen, who plays Jimmy in *Thelma & Louise*, indicates that such ideas of male honor may continue to carry power today. The actor noted in an interview that he thought his character Jimmy would have subscribed to these beliefs and that he considered Jimmy the type of man who would not have stayed with a woman if he knew she had been raped.[17]

With her screenplay, Khouri redirects the genre by featuring rape and sexual assault from the point of view of the two white female characters. After Louise kills Harlan and they drive away, the women reflect on what they should do, with Thelma suggesting they tell the police Harlan tried to rape her. Louise reminds her that a "hundred" people at the bar saw her dancing "cheek to cheek" with him. Because of that, no one is ever going to believe her story, she insists. "We don't live in that kind of a world." Increasingly distraught about the murder of Harlan, Louise asks Thelma to pull the car over and then vomits on the side of the road. After Louise collects herself and helps Thelma clean the blood off her face, they stop at a diner to figure out their next steps. While Louise looks at a road map in silence, Thelma tries to stop crying and then tells Louise sarcastically, "I'll say one thing. This is some vacation." Mocking Harlan's earlier comments in the parking lot, she says, "We're sure having a good time. This is real fun." Louise quickly looks up. "If you were so concerned about having such a good time, we wouldn't be sitting here right now." Shocked at the outburst, Thelma asks, "Just what is that supposed to mean? . . . So this is all my fault, is it?"

While she refuses to be blamed for the assault, Thelma also knows it's likely she'll be ignored and dismissed if she reports the crime and that her previous interactions with Harlan will be unfairly held against her. These circumstances render her "unrapeable," to use a term developed by feminists and particularly feminists of color to critique the ways some women's rape allegations are discredited and the ways their actions or identity somehow make them undeserving of belief, support, or protection in the larger culture.[18] This sentiment appears in *Duel in the Sun* (King Vidor and Otto Brower, 1946), a Western that features a love triangle between two brothers and Pearl Chavez (Jennifer Jones, a white actress), who is described in the film as a "half-breed girl from down along the border . . . herself a wild flower . . . quick to blossom and early to die." For at least one male character in the movie, Pearl's mixed heritage positions her as "unrapeable," as if a situation or circumstance could exist where a woman would somehow forfeit her right to give or withhold consent.

In *The Right to Sex: Feminism in the Twenty-First Century*, Amia Srinivasan examines the false belief that some women are "unrapeable" and the thinking that tries to exonerate men who rape. In her study, Srinivasan also counters arguments that suggest certain men— and here we could include the character Harlan—are somehow not in a position to "know better" about their actions. Those who claim ignorance on the part of men, she argues, are "in denial of what men have seen and heard."[19] Instead, we should recognize that these men "have chosen not to listen because it has suited them not to do so, because the norms of masculinity dictate that their pleasure takes priority, because all around them other men have been doing the same."[20] The disdain for consent, along with male entitlement and sexual privilege, means that a man like Harlan would probably not be arrested for attempted rape, that testimony from a woman such as Thelma would probably not be believed, and that a figure like Louise would probably be arrested and jailed for firing the shot that killed him.

In the film, the gun takes on tremendous meaning and consequence for the two women, putting in place elements that will forever change the course of their lives. It is introduced early in the movie, when Thelma throws it into her travel bag, almost as an afterthought. Just as the women drive off for their weekend getaway, Thelma nervously pulls it out of her purse, holding it with the tip of her fingers. She then hands the gun to Louise and asks her to keep it safe, explaining that it might come in handy if they need to protect themselves from "psycho killers, bears, snakes." At first Louise refuses, thinking that carrying a firearm with them on their trip is a very bad idea. She eventually agrees to take care of it, partly to keep her friend from frantically waving it in the air and possibly shooting someone. The real danger, however, comes in the form of a predatory man who dances with Thelma at the bar and grooms her with drinks, a man who already has a reputation at the Silver Bullet for assaulting women and who feels entitled to ignore Thelma's protests.

The women's deep reluctance to carry the gun makes them somewhat unusual outlaws in the history of the Western. Indeed, we could argue that few Westerns feature main characters who lack experience with guns at the level they do or are as reluctant to handle firearms as they are. In Westerns, guns play a significant role in defining the main character. "Every Western hero is in a sense a gunfighter," Edward Buscombe explains, and "a conflict with firearms is the almost invariable conclusion to a Western film."[21] Being a skilled gunman is often crucial to the genre's plotline, and guns themselves are frequently linked to understandings of American rights and freedoms. Buscombe builds on Eric Mottram's argument that in US history, the right to bear arms is tied to ideas about individualism, and in the Western, the gun often symbolizes the right of individual Americans to protect themselves against enemies.[22] Yet the gun also reveals contradictions, as Buscombe notes, especially concerning the autonomous westerner whose self-reliant identity actually depends on the firearm, itself a symbol of the technology and modern changes that perennially threaten the settler West.[23]

At times, Westerns take a critical view of violence and gunplay by showing how the use of force negatively impacts the main character and the community. Sometimes titles of films reference their violent characters—for example, *The Gunfighter* (1950) and *The Shootist* (1976), both of which raise ethical questions about killing and the problems that emerge when such violence is introduced into the community. In a related way, Westerns such as *Shane* (George Stevens, 1953) feature a cowboy hero who may have fled his brutal past but is drawn back to a life of violence after he is called upon to protect the community from a deadly threat. A number of critics have pointed to the complexities of the hero's relationship to violence. Andrew Patrick Nelson notes, for instance, how a reformed gunman in the Western may attempt to "turn in his pistol for a plow," but that such efforts typically do not succeed. While settler society may have requested his services for protection, violence can have no place in that world. By the end of the film, as Nelson explains, the hero is "doomed to a life of endless wandering," forced to exist outside the very community he fought to keep safe.[24] At the closing of such a story, the hero rides away from the town he made safe, like Shane does, or is left in an ambiguous place, as Ethan Edwards is in *The Searchers*, consigned to the margins of the family and community he previously sought to restore.

Female gunslingers often add a different element of complexity to the Western's treatment of violence. In *Johnny Guitar* (Nicholas Ray, 1954), Joan Crawford plays a saloonkeeper and skilled shooter named Vienna who must hold her own against her romantic and business rival Emma Small (Mercedes McCambridge). Emma is responsible for organizing a lynch mob to capture the outlaw responsible for killing her brother in

Figure 22. Vienna, the female gunslinger and saloon owner in *Johnny Guitar* (1954)

a holdup. Emma's other goals involve preventing the development of the railroad, which threatens her livelihood, and eliminating her prime competitor, Vienna. A formidable presence in the community, Vienna is known for violating gender norms by assuming the role and behavior of men. "I've never seen a woman who was more a man. She thinks like one, acts like one, and sometimes makes me feel like I'm not," says one of her male employees in the saloon.

Throughout the film, Emma taunts her female rival, publicly calling Vienna a "tramp" in front of others. We learn that before Vienna was a saloon owner, she was employed as a sex worker in a bar. Later, she gives a memorable speech about the sexual double standards women often face. "A man can lie, even kill, but as long as he hangs on to his pride, he's still a man. All a woman has to do is slip once, and she's a tramp. Must be a great comfort to you to be a man," she tells her love interest, Johnny (Sterling Hayden). Vienna may act like a man, but she is ultimately not treated like one in the film. As if to balance out her sexual and social power, the movie takes its title from the name of the male love interest rather than the leading character.

In other ways, too, the film curtails the female's strengths as a gunslinger, which helps reinstate the gender status quo. While she is skilled with firearms and does not shy away from confrontation, Vienna confesses to Johnny that she is hesitant to actually kill anyone. In the closing scene featuring a shootout between the two female rivals, Vienna fires a fatal shot at Emma, finally managing to overcome her reluctance to kill in self-defense. Her determination to protect herself from an outside threat is undercut, however, when Johnny comes to her aid, leading her away from the scene in a gesture that restores the sexual order and neutralizes Vienna's power.

*Forty Guns* (Samuel Fuller, 1957) also complicates the treatment of women, violence, and firearms. Throughout the film, a number of scenes feature male and female characters handling and stroking guns in humorous, over-the-top sequences that treat weapons as phallic symbols and gunplay as a thinly veiled stand-in for sex. In doing so, the story introduces female sexuality and power only to contain these disruptive elements by the end of the movie. In the film, Barbara Stanwyck plays Jessica Drummond, a "high-ridin' woman with a whip" who loves fast horses and does whatever it takes to protect her ranch and family from the forces that threaten them. While she is a self-possessed and capable ranchwoman, Jessica eventually falls for Griff Bonnell (Barry Sullivan), the lawman responsible for killing her renegade brother Brockie (John Ericson). She maintains her power and autonomy until the last scene, when she throws

Figure 23. Gunslinger Jessica with her firearm in *Forty Guns* (1957)

it all aside, running down the road and calling out to the lawman before joining him as he rides out of town, having completed his job of restoring peace and order to the community.

*The Belle Starr Story* (Piero Cristofani and Lina Wertmüller, 1968) likewise features a female gunslinger who threatens to disrupt gender hierarchies but whose power is eventually contained through heterosexual romance.[25] Elsa Martinelli plays the title role, a female card shark who smokes cigars, wears men's clothing, and rescues women in need. "Say, you must be that gal dressed up like a fellow that everyone's been talking about," one character exclaims upon seeing her. The story sends Belle on a number of dangerous adventures that include riding alongside a gang of armed bandits who wreak havoc across the West; saving a woman from the hangman's noose at the last moment; escaping from a shootout in a saloon where she is outnumbered by a gang of villains; and maneuvering out of a marriage with a much older man, an arrangement set up by her immoral uncle, a sexual predator who is responsible for killing her parents. The film extends some of the standard plotlines of the genre in

Figure 24. Belle Starr, a spaghetti Western gunslinger, in *The Belle Starr Story* (1968)

interesting ways but does not fully empower its female lead, whose gender and sexual transgressions are continually reigned in at key moments when she surrenders to her male love interest and allows him to take charge.

*Hannie Caulder* (Burt Kennedy, 1971) features a female gunslinger, played by Latinx actress Raquel Welch, whose husband is killed by the Clemens brothers (Ernest Borgnine, Jack Elam, and Strother Martin), a gang of inept but violent bank robbers who rape her, burn down her house, and steal her horses. When a bounty hunter named Thomas (Robert Culp) shows up at her property, she uses the opportunity to learn how to handle a gun in order to avenge the crimes committed against her. With all her personal items lost in the fire, Hannie spends much of the movie wearing only a wool blanket. It covers little of her body but resembles the poncho worn by the mysterious gunfighter played by Clint Eastwood in various spaghetti Westerns directed by Sergio Leone.[26] In addition to costume, *Hannie Caulder* shows its links to Italian Westerns through its musical score by Ennio Morricone and its production in Almería, Spain.

As we learn in the film, however, the female gunslinger Hannie is no spaghetti Western hero, her identity as a woman preventing her from

Figure 25. Thomas mansplains to Hannie how to shoot a gun in *Hannie Caulder* (1971)

occupying that iconic role. Often expressing concern about women getting the upper hand, the movie serves more as a reaction to the struggles for expanded roles and opportunities associated with the women's movement of the late 1960s and '70s than an endorsement of social change. "Fine-lookin' woman," one man says of Hannie. "She wants to be a man," Thomas replies. "Never make it," the other man says. "No, not likely," he agrees. In shootouts when she confronts her enemies, including the vicious Clemens brothers, Hannie hesitates to kill. After Thomas is knifed to death by an outlaw, she hears his lessons about always firing twice echoing in her head. "Again, Hannie, again," the voice tells her. Although Hannie gains the skills to become an effective gunslinger, her agency is undercut when she hands authority over to men and when she requires their presence or assistance in avenging the crimes committed against her. The perplexing and underdeveloped closing scene also features Hannie leaving town with a mysterious gunman who has appeared in earlier moments of the film, but whose identity and purpose are never revealed in the story.

In contrast, *Thelma & Louise* offers a departure from these plotlines in that it doesn't empty women of their power or depict them as dependent on men for their agency and authority. Khouri's script provides a different take, featuring runaway women breaking out of and escaping the rule of men, moving toward a possible queer future that suggests new freedoms and possibilities. Departing from standard treatments of gender and power in the Western, *Thelma & Louise* avoids narrow definitions of violence. In an important way, the film recognizes how violence itself operates in many forms, as a physical, ideological, and political force.

As such, the movie connects with recent work by feminist scholars who address epistemic violence and epistemic injustice. Postcolonial critic Gayatri Spivak, for instance, defines epistemic violence as the damage that results when less powerful voices are silenced or when their truths are disregarded by the dominant culture.[27] Feminist philosopher Miranda Fricker builds on Spivak's ideas by developing the concept of epistemic injustice to address the "deflated level of credibility" often assigned to a speaker due to larger social prejudices about authority and believability. Such actions wrong a person "in their capacity as a subject of knowledge and thus in a capacity essential to human value."[28] In the film, Thelma and Louise acknowledge such forms of violence and injustice when they realize they would most likely be blamed if they went to the police and that their voices would probably be discounted or discredited if they reported the attempted rape by Harlan or the earlier rape in Texas.

Drawing on the concepts of epistemic violence and injustice, feminist philosopher Kate Abramson examines the problems posed by gaslighting, a type of epistemic injustice that aims to silence or discredit the voices of others. The term originates from the 1944 film *Gaslight* (George Cukor) about a manipulative and controlling husband who tries to convince his wife that she is losing her mind. In particular, he lies to her about the cause of a flickering light, a deception that is part of his larger plan to make his wife question her sanity so he can claim her inheritance. Building from this film plot, Abramson and other critics frame gaslighting as a tactic of emotional manipulation meant to confuse or convince someone—typically a woman— that their understanding of reality is false. It is not merely disagreement, but involves convincing someone that they should not take themselves seriously or trust their ability to reason. Gaslighting is meant to persuade a person that their own thinking or sense of the world is somehow unbelievable and unreliable.[29]

Abramson notes that gaslighting is typically a gendered phenomenon, with women more likely to be victims of manipulation and men the perpetrators. Gaslighting relies on women having internalized sexist norms and typically emerges in moments when women protest against sexism itself.[30] Its strategies include "flatly" denying and "radically minimizing" the critique initially launched against the gaslighter, defining the other person as "crazy for being upset," and insisting that she is not simply wrong but "oversensitive" and in "no condition to judge whether she is wrong or mistaken."[31] The goal involves domination and the maintenance of the existing power structure by determining the acceptable way of knowing.[32]

Recently, the concept of gaslighting received greater attention through the #MeToo movement and news coverage of various sexual assault and rape charges leveled against powerful men in Hollywood. Although Khouri wrote her script before feminist studies of gaslighting had circulated widely, *Thelma & Louise* offers insightful examples of this disempowering behavior. Abramson's observation that gaslighting is a tool used by those with an "inability to tolerate even the possibility of challenge" goes far in explaining Darryl's actions in the film.[33] Khouri's screenplay depicts

Darryl as imagining himself to be the "king of their tiny little castle."[34] He constantly asserts his power by berating and belittling his wife. More than once, Louise expresses her disdain for Thelma's husband; likewise, neither Hal nor J. D. think very highly of him. As confirmed by people who know Darryl, Thelma has very good reasons for leaving her marriage. Preoccupied with his looks and professional appearances, Darryl grooms himself excessively and brags about his job as regional director of a carpet store, which he claims keeps him from coming home early most Friday nights. Thelma is on to his lies but is careful not to anger her husband, knowing how much Darryl does not want to be contradicted and how quickly he can become irate.

When anyone counters his version of events, Darryl pauses meaningfully and blinks his eyes slowly in a display of exaggerated disbelief, a gesture that adds humor to the film while also showing his intolerance of other viewpoints. As Abramson notes, an "unbearable anxiety" about being questioned makes the gaslighting perpetrator want to destroy the "independent perspective and moral standing" of their victims.[35] "What is being expressed is a deep interpersonal need for assent, an intolerance for being challenged, and the desire to destroy the very possibility of disagreement, all of which are taking the form of a manipulative demand," she explains.[36]

When Darryl lies to Thelma about his reasons for staying late at work or calls her "crazy" for not wanting to return home, he's gaslighting her. When Harlan tells Louise in the parking lot of the Silver Bullet that he's just having a little fun with Thelma even though she has not consented to having sex with him and is in fact crying, he uses gaslighting to make excuses for his physical force and violence. Detective Hal Slocumb also engages in gaslighting when he insists that he is an ally trying to help the

Figure 26. Darryl gaslights in *Thelma & Louise* (1991)

two women. While he may have sympathy for the female outlaws, Hal
feels bound to his job and gains their confidence by showing concern for
them. When he tells Louise on the phone he knows what happened to
her in Texas, Hal seems to be expressing interest in connecting with her.
Yet he does so ultimately to keep her talking long enough to allow law
enforcement to determine their location.

Work by feminist philosophers likewise helps us understand the backlash that occurs when Thelma and Louise try to escape the restrictions
of gender by refusing to provide the emotional care and labor men have
become accustomed to receiving from them. The affective economy of
Thelma's relationship with Darryl means that she gives in to his demands
most of the time. When she withholds emotional care from the marriage,
he typically reacts in anger. In *Down Girl: The Logic of Misogyny*, Kate
Manne highlights what often follows in the wake of women's refusals.
Darryl fits her description of the entitled man who "views and treats certain women in his orbit . . . as owing him . . . her distinctively human
services and capacities, much more than vice versa."[37] At times, Thelma's

openness and care for others ends up placing the two women in deeper trouble. We see this in the scene at the motel, when Thelma explains to J. D. why they are fleeing and tells him their plans about escaping to Mexico. Believing himself entitled to take what he needs, J. D. absconds with the women's money. After his arrest, J. D. tells the police where they are heading. Louise finally insists that Thelma stop being "so open" with others and stop sharing so much of herself. "We're fugitives now. Let's behave that way."

Elaborating on the significance of women's emotional labor and care work, Manne argues that it is often "required" for women to show men "moral respect, approval, admiration, deference, and gratitude, as well as moral attention, sympathy, and concern." In situations where she is "withholding from him the good will he may be accustomed to receiving from her," he may "seek payback, revenge, retribution" or resort to what Manne calls the "smackdown."[38] As she notes, these instances foreground how much the man in question may be dependent on the woman and may even be "in some sense reliant on her good will to maintain his tenuous sense of self or self-worth."[39]

A scene with Louise foregrounds these dynamics. Early in the film as she packs her bags for the road trip, Louise comes across a picture of Jimmy and turns it upside down on the table, a gesture indicating that perhaps their relationship has finally run its course. The moment may also express her refusal to continue offering the care work she has granted so far, a kind of emotional labor that Jimmy himself does not provide in the relationship. Later at the motel, when it becomes clear the relationship is over and Louise is not planning on explaining the situation to him, Jimmy explodes in anger, violently turning over furniture and breaking property as Louise heads for the door.

Figure 27. Thelma takes aim at a police officer in *Thelma & Louise* (1991)

Toward the end of the film, Thelma and Louise parody the affective roles women are frequently assigned when they offer over-the-top apologies to the policeman before locking him in the trunk of his patrol car. As noted in chapter 1, upon hearing the man speak about his family in a plea for mercy, Thelma gives him some advice, telling the man to be good to his family and treat them well, "especially his wife." Thelma holds herself up as an example of what could happen when men abuse their power, implying that years of gaslighting, mistreatment, and unequal care relations have the power to turn a good woman bad.

While Thelma and Louise experience backlash for withholding the emotional labor expected from the men in their lives, they also engage in what are often considered to be inappropriate affects or emotional responses. Some critiques of the film focus on the women's expression of anger, rage, and resentment at the injustices they encounter. In her essay "The Aptness of Anger," Amia Srinivasan examines a related moral argument about anger, specifically the idea that anger should be avoided due to the counterproductive effects that may follow in its wake. As she contends, however, there is "more to anger, normatively speaking, than its effects. Even if anger is counterproductive we can still ask: is it the fitting response to the way the world is? Is it, in other words, apt?"[40] Srinivasan argues that while there is some truth to the argument about the underside of anger, namely that it may make things worse for the individual, she critiques these claims by pointing to moments where anger would nonetheless be an appropriate response.[41] She observes that the "false dichotomy" between "reason and anger" is an example of affective injustice.[42] Such instances shift the context for the person's anger, from the immoral act itself to the person who was harmed. The argument that anger is counterproductive *"explains away"* the anger, making it a character flaw rather than an appropriate reaction to the experience of injustice.[43] In this way, a "moral violation" emerges when anger is ignored or cast off as being counterproductive in the struggle for justice.[44] Srinivasan points out the problem that appears when people confess they feel "nothing in response to those moral wrongs" when forms of anger are involved.[45] Such responses falsely imply that the wronged person should put up with unethical or damaging behavior and that what are deemed to be inappropriate affects or emotions are somehow worse than the offensive behavior itself.

After the truck driver in *Thelma & Louise* gestures crudely to the women and harasses them on the road, the women respond in anger, convincing him to pull over to the side of the road while pretending they're interested in having sex with him. The driver takes off his wedding ring, hops out of the truck, and does a little jig, thinking he's going to get some action. When the women use the opportunity to tell him he is being rude to them, the truck driver laughs it off as if they're joking. "I bet you even called us beavers on your CB radio, didn't you?" Thelma asks. "Damn, I hate that. I hate being called a beaver, don't you?" she asks Louise. The truck driver's lighthearted mood turns to confusion when the women ask why he believes he can get away with this kind of behavior. "We think you have really bad manners," Louise tells him. "We were just wondering where you think you get off behaving like that to women you don't even know. . . . We think you should apologize."

When the truck driver refuses, the women pull out their guns and blow up his tanker. Their response admittedly is a moment of excessive violence meant to signal the final straw or tipping point for the women, with the explosion of the truck operating as a kind of wish fulfillment that uses a deliberately exaggerated response to heighten the stakes of the film and foreground the issues women often face on the road. We could also argue that the scene takes the idea of white women's "civilizing" role in the Western to a new level. Here the women blow up the trucker driver's vehicle because he has bad manners and is being insulting to them. In that sense, the man must be taught a lesson. In the logic of the Western, he must be "civilized."

In another way, the moment helps place *Thelma & Louise* in the tradition of the action-adventure movie, which typically draws on violence as a means for engaging social critique. Yvonne Tasker addresses this point in her discussion of the movie, writing that "action films operate in part to dramatize transgression," or the "breaking of official codes of the law" and as a way of critiquing "codes of social behavior" themselves.[46] As a film that explores "limits and transgressions," *Thelma & Louise* often relies on structures of fantasy rather than elements of reality. It thus "operates within a different set of terms," Tasker argues, within what we might regard as "utopian."[47]

Negative reviews often call out this explosive scene with the truck driver, directing focus away from the trucker driver's actions while

Figure 28. Teaching manners to a truck driver in *Thelma & Louise* (1991)

condemning the film as a whole, as if the movie were somehow suggesting that disgruntled female viewers should immediately go out and respond in the same way—blow up semitrucks if male drivers sexually harass them. Perhaps in an effort to preempt such arguments, the film makes a joke about the media's potential influence on viewers' behavior. After they blow up the truck, Louise turns to her friend and asks how she learned to shoot a gun like that. Thelma replies that she learned it from watching TV. Meanwhile, the truck driver responds with fury, calling the women "bitches" and shaking his hands in the air. His curses are meant to draw attention away from his own transgressions and to place responsibility onto the women, the "bitches" who are overly malicious and inappropriately spiteful and who should know that it is better to put up with sexist and demeaning treatment than to get angry about it.[48]

The trucker's response also highlights something else in the film involving language and violence. Before the explosion, the movie lingers over the driver as he wags his tongue in a lewd gesture that matches the coarseness of his words. Marita Sturken argues that language carries tremendous power in the film, referencing the moment when Louise shoots Harlan because he's "unremorseful" and because of what he says to her. Sturken also points to the scene when the women blow up the truck "not simply" because the driver "has acted toward them in a crude and lecherous manner, but because he refuses to apologize for his behavior." She notes that while the women have become outlaws in the film, they "still retain certain codes about what constitutes decent human behavior," which in this case includes the treatment of words and speech itself.[49]

To build on these observations, we could argue that the rules of behavior Thelma and Louise seem to be following are also codes of conduct guiding the Western, a genre that often gives importance to wordplay and language. While critics over the years tend to focus on the laconic cowboy or man of few words as a central figure in the Western, Lee Clark Mitchell notes how "rhetorical mastery" and "verbal craftmanship" are often crucial elements in the genre, tracing how skilled wordsmithing plays out in the example of *The Virginian*, Owen Wister's classic 1902 novel whose hero frequently "triumphs not through bullets but with words."[50] In *Thelma & Louise*, language also reveals character while wordplay itself becomes a weapon for power and control. Men in the film are not taciturn but speak a great deal. Throughout the movie, they lie, they interrupt, they say insulting things, and they deliberately mislead the two women with their false talk. Men's speech in this Western is clearly not to be trusted.

Likewise, the language of men is frequently a cause or an intensifier of violence in the movie. We see this in Darryl's endless fabrications and his treatment of Thelma, who leaves their home in order to escape her husband's abuse and neglect. We see it in Harlan's smooth talking and grooming of Thelma and his dismissive comments and insults toward Louise. We also note it in J. D.'s playful and convincing lessons about robbery "done right" and Hal's phone calls that seem supportive but eventually enable the FBI to pinpoint the women's whereabouts near the end of the film. Finally, we see it in the scene with the truck driver, who not only demeans Thelma and Louise with his words but wags his tongue at them in a sexually degrading way. "I mean, really! That business with your tongue. What is that? That's disgustin'," Thelma admonishes him.

The movie goes far in critiquing the multiple forms of violence that disrupt the lives of the female protagonists, including physical, sexual, epistemic, and linguistic. Yet *Thelma & Louise* also presents problems along these lines that deserve further attention. The sequence involving the African American cyclist (Noel Walcott), for instance, has garnered debate among scholars. Some viewers recognize the character as a potential ally and unexpected partner in crime for the two women after he takes a break near the patrol car, smokes some weed, and blows it into the air hole of the trunk where the police officer is being held against his will. Moving away from these readings, Sharon Willis notes the violence of erasure. She builds on Toni Morrison's argument in *Playing in the Dark: Whiteness and the Literary Imagination* regarding the ways a "thunderous, theatrical presence of black surrogacy" often appears in American literary history only to be rendered "meaning-less," a development that works to deracialize the story and American history itself. Examining the film's treatment of the African American cyclist, Willis notes we never hear the character speak in the movie and that his presence remains a "mute, resistant image" in a film that rarely remarks on race or discusses whiteness itself.[51]

Such allegiances are also undercut after Thelma trades in her white frilly clothing for black attire, a change that signals her renegade status in the Western. Critic Bernie Cook notes that a turning point in the movie

Figure 29. African American cyclist in *Thelma & Louise* (1991)

features Thelma wearing a black T-shirt with a skull and a Confederate flag across the front.[52] Such attire is meant to position Thelma as outside the law, yet in featuring this image, the clothing uncritically references a violent history of racial oppression, the institution of slavery, and ongoing structures of white supremacy. Ultimately, the use of a racist symbol undercuts Thelma's position in the film and eliminates possibilities for developing cross-racial allyship or intersectional feminism.[53]

Other problems regarding race and nation shape the movie as well. Part of the movie was filmed in Monument Valley, a cinematic location often associated with Western movies. As Audrey Goodman reminds us, however, the Western typically disregards the location's identity as "Diné land," a site that carries a different meaning that escapes the Western and resists being incorporated into its "popular panoramic form," namely "the meaning of a home and relations among kin across generations."[54] In addition to Monument Valley, *Thelma & Louise* was filmed in Utah on land that has been the ancestral home of the Navajo, the Zuni, the Hopi, the Southern Ute, the Ute Indian Tribe of the Uintah and Ouray Reservation,

Figure 30. Native American diners in *Thelma & Louise* (1991)

the Paiute Indian Tribe of Utah, and the Kaibab Band of Paiute Indians.[55] Yet the film features no central Indigenous characters, and the only scene that includes Indigenous people appears in the brief sequence at the motel diner where Native American customers are seated in the background but have no significant role or dialogue in the movie.[56]

Likewise, the sequences filmed near Moab, Utah, become meaningful in discussing other structures of violence in the West. A former uranium mining town, Moab was part of the nation's Cold War nuclear landscape. Geographers, including Mike Davis and Valerie Kuletz, have written extensively about the fallout across the militarized West, the ecological violence of resource extraction, and the fate of downwinders, including some Indigenous populations whose traditional homelands were located near nuclear test zones.[57]

Here we might also recall Ann Putnam's argument mentioned earlier about the gendered use of force and restrictions the women continually encounter on their journey. *Thelma & Louise* lays bare the violence of Western masculinity and how the demands of the genre often mean

Figure 31. Exchanging jewelry for a hat in a ghost town of the toxic West in
*Thelma & Louise* (1991)

that complex moral situations are resolved through the use of brute force.
Thelma and Louise move through spaces that are, to quote Putnam again,
"awash in waves of pumping testosterone" as well as "spouting steam,
spraying planes, spilling hoses, pumping oil riggers, and men pumping
iron and pumping gas."[58] These scenes exemplify forms of toxic masculinity while also providing visual evidence of what critic Sylvan Goldberg
calls "extractive masculinity," a gender expression that emerges out of the
"violent legacy of an androcentric culture" in the West. As he explains, the
term recognizes "sexual violence" in conjunction with ecological violence,
particularly the "harm resulting" from histories of resource extraction
across the region.[59]

In his work on ecocriticism and the Western, Goldberg builds on
arguments Stacy Alaimo has made about the appearance of a "high carbon masculinity" in recent US culture. In *Exposed: Environmental Politics
and Pleasures in Posthuman Times*, Alaimo describes an "impervious" and
"swaggering" attitude of denial about environmental destruction in general

Figure 32. The carbon footprint of *Thelma & Louise* (1991)

and climate change in particular that is often framed by a performance of hypermasculinity and excessive energy use. Patterns of consumerism, for instance, have seen SUVs and pickup trucks increasing in size over the years. Likewise, the "rolling coal" movement where trucks are equipped to use more rather than less gas in order to emit visible black clouds of soot—often directed toward groups that they revile—reveals much about problems of toxic gender expression in contemporary America.[60]

Extending these ideas, we may also wish to reflect more fully on what drives the movement toward freedom and liberation in the film and how sustainable these solutions actually are. In this way, the women's fossil-fueled journey toward freedom in a '66 Thunderbird may be reevaluated along with the explosion of the semitruck as instances of the environmental footprint of road movies themselves. These examples complicate the feminism of the movie. As Claire Colebrook points out—updating the second wave slogan—not only is the personal political here, but "the personal is geological."[61]

At times, the film does express ambivalence about these toxic practices.

We see this ambivalence in scenes showing vehicles with their exhaust blasting across the road that the women have to maneuver away from or the sequence featuring the crop-dusting airplane that dumps pesticides onto the back roads where the women seek refuge. As such, viewers may wish to extend discussions of violence in the film by examining how ecology, racial identity, and knowledge are all crucial and intersecting topics to consider in assessing the Western. Restoring deeper understandings of how energy, power, and freedom overlap and complicate the world of Thelma and Louise, we may better assess the ways multiple forms of violence also work to limit and restrict sustainable lives in the film.

## CONCLUSION | Beyond the Abyss

When Callie Khouri won the Oscar for best original screenplay in 1992, her acceptance speech at the Academy Awards ceremony expressed optimism about new possibilities for female filmmakers and her sense that things were finally opening up for women in Hollywood. "For everybody that wanted to see a happy ending for Thelma and Louise," she proclaimed, "to me this is it."[1] As Khouri's speech suggested, the Academy's recognition of her screenplay was a hopeful sign that a cinematic future existed beyond the abyss for strong and rebellious women like her two main characters.

With the passage of time, the movie has remained popular with many audiences even as it serves as a reminder of what is yet to be achieved. On the twenty-fifth anniversary of the film's release, the *Atlantic* featured a story by Megan Garber that proclaimed, "Thelma & Louise Holds Up Well—a Little Too Well." In her essay, Garber notes that in 2016, the movie still "feels relevant" in terms of sexual politics—especially so today with the impact of Dobbs. While we might recognize and celebrate *Thelma & Louise* for its staying power regarding gender and sexuality, the author cautions that this is actually not a good thing. For Garber, the movie's continued relevance signals the way there is still much more work to be done in struggles for equality. Yet the film's staying power, as I noted previously, is not strong when it comes to racism, settler colonialism, and ecology.[2]

*Thelma & Louise* raised expectations for many viewers, adding urgency to the push for more compelling representations of women on screen and greater participation of women in key positions in film production. Although the movie drew attention to issues surrounding gender, sexuality, and inequality, it would be some time before notable change took hold in the industry. In the more than three decades since the film's release, women who work as screenwriters, directors, and actors still face an uphill battle and continue to lag behind men in the opportunities available to them in the industry. In terms of other workplace issues, it would take Hollywood more than a decade to feel the impact of the #MeToo movement, which began in 2006 when African American activist Tarana Burke first used the term "Me Too" to draw attention to the prevalence of sexual assault. In 2017, the hashtag #MeToo went viral and shook the movie industry, resulting in a number of high-profile rape and sexual assault allegations against powerful men in the industry.[3]

*Thelma & Louise* saw tremendous popularity upon its release and has remained an important film over the years, contributing in particular to a revisionist cycle of the Western featuring stories about women and their struggles in the region. Recent Western films in this category include *The Ballad of Little Jo* (1993), *Bad Girls* (1994), *The Quick and the Dead* (1995), *Gang of Roses* (2003), *Bandidas* (2006), *Meek's Cutoff* (2010), *The Homesman* (2014), *Jane Got a Gun* (2015), and *Woman Walks Ahead* (2017). In television, numerous Westerns have also appeared that feature strong roles for women, including *Dr. Quinn Medicine Woman* (1993–1998), *Buffalo Girls* (1995), *Godless* (2017), *Strange Empire* (2014–2015), *Wynonna Earp* (2016–2021), *Westworld* (2016–2022), and *The English* (2022).

In assessing the film's influence, it is indeed difficult to imagine that certain movies and television shows could have been made without *Thelma & Louise*. The film helped inspire the production of more diverse stories about the West, revealing the degree to which, as Neil Campbell argues, the "mythic frame" often "surrounding and encircling the West, can be interfered with in order to demonstrate alternative ways of thinking and being."[4] In the 1998 film *Smoke Signals* directed by Chris Eyre (Cheyenne/Arapaho), for instance, a memorable sequence features an updated take on *Thelma & Louise*. Set on the Coeur d'Alene Reservation, *Smoke Signals* references the earlier film in a scene featuring two Indigenous women—Velma and Lucy (Michelle St. John and Elaine Miles)—who take off on their own free-spirited road trip. The sequence shows the Native American women driving backward in their car, which mirrors a scene in *Thelma & Louise* when Louise puts her convertible in reverse in order to avoid another confrontation. In *Smoke Signals*, the main conflict is not about escaping the threat of predatory or abusive men but instead about addressing the problems posed by colonialism, racism, and economic precarity, as symbolized by the run-down car that will only drive in reverse.

With an ending that sends its two female characters over the abyss and that queers the Western, the road film, the buddy movie, and the screwball comedy in the process, *Thelma & Louise* also seems to have helped open up new avenues for developing LGBTQ+ story lines. While queer desire appears just briefly in the movie and, as Anneke Smelik argues, "can only be expressed in a kiss" at the very end of the film, we could argue that *Thelma & Louise* paved the way for subsequent Westerns such as *Brokeback Mountain* (Ang Lee, 2005) and *The Power of the Dog* (Jane Campion, 2021).[5]

Figure 33. Velma and Lucy on the road in *Smoke Signals* (1998)

Based on a 1997 short story by Annie Proulx that was first published in the *New Yorker*, *Brokeback Mountain* had a budget of only $14 million but went on to gross more than $178 million at the box office. Featuring Jake Gyllenhaal and Heath Ledger in the lead roles, *Brokeback Mountain* is set in Wyoming in 1963 and tells the story of a doomed love affair between two cowboys, Jack and Ennis. Like *Thelma & Louise*, the movie also experienced backlash and controversy about its subject matter. Nonetheless, it went on to win numerous awards, including Oscars for best director for Ang Lee and best adapted screenplay for Larry McMurtry and Diana Ossana.[6]

*The Power of the Dog* is based on a 1967 novel by Thomas Savage. Set in Montana in 1925, the film tells the story of two brothers and the challenges that fracture their relationship when the younger sibling George (Jesse Plemons) marries a widow named Rose (Kirsten Dunst) and moves her and her son, Peter (Kodi Smit-McPhee), to the ranch. Unhappy about the change, the older brother Phil (Benedict Cumberbatch) makes life difficult for his sister-in-law while terrorizing her son, who is gay. The film addresses toxic masculinity and internalized homophobia, ending with Peter taking revenge on Phil, whom he murders by secretly poisoning him with anthrax. Filmed during the COVID-19 pandemic, *The Power of the Dog* had a limited theatrical release and was later released for streaming on Netflix. The movie was nominated and won numerous film awards, including an Oscar for best director for Jane Campion.[7]

The impact of *Thelma & Louise* may also be seen in Westerns that feature female gunslingers and that address concerns about race, nation, sexuality, and power. The 2006 movie *Bandidas* (Joachim Rønning and Espen Sandberg) offers a humorous take on gender, violence, and the Western. The movie was cowritten by Luc Besson, who previously directed the French action thriller *La Femme Nikita* (1990), and Robert Mark Kamen, who wrote the scripts for the *Karate Kid* movies. *Bandidas* stars Penélope Cruz (as María) and Selma Hayek (as Sara) in a comic Western set in Mexico at the turn of the twentieth century. When a US-owned railroad company threatens local landowners, María and Sara join forces to protect their community and stop the incursion.

Like *Thelma & Louise*, the film upsets a number of gendered conventions in the Western. For one, daughters replace fathers in the job of avenging assault and murder. The women also become the hostage takers when they hold a man named Quentin (Steve Zahn) against his will, tie him to a bed, place him in sexually compromising situations, and then threaten to go public with the images they've created unless he agrees to help them. While lessons about guns in the Western often serve as a metaphor for women's sexual initiation, *Bandidas* casts a woman in the role of instructor when Sara takes the lead in teaching María how to seduce a man, using the kidnapped Quentin as her test subject. Although at times the film is a bit ambiguous about its political commitments, it

Figure 34. Female gunslingers in *Bandidas* (2006)

draws attention to patriarchal themes in the Western while critiquing US empire and capitalist expansion. The movie also reminds us that many of the lands featured in *Thelma & Louise* were once part of Mexico.

*Thelma & Louise* draws on a number of cinematic forms. In this way, some of its impact may be seen in *Wynonna Earp* (2016–2021), a recent TV series about a female gunslinger that brings together different genres in surprising ways. Airing on the Syfy station, the show is a Canadian American production created by writer and producer Emily Andras and based on a comic book series by Beau Smith. Classified by some critics as a "weird Western" that combines other genres including fantasy, horror, and science fiction, *Wynonna Earp* offers a new take on the legendary story of Wyatt Earp and Doc Holliday. The show places historical and present-day events in a supernatural context while imagining ways for previously sidelined characters to take center stage in the Western.[8] Set in the town of Purgatory, which is haunted by various undead demon outlaws, the series follows the titular protagonist (played by Melanie Scrofano) as she seeks justice in the West.

The show depicts its main character as a descendent of the famed Wyatt Earp, a modern female gunslinger who offers biting comebacks to the sexist insults she receives while also managing to stave off threats to her community. *Wynonna Earp* likewise helped queer the Western with the introduction of the character Nicole (Katherine Barrell), who becomes the love interest of Waverly, Wynonna's younger sister (Dominique Provost-Chalkley). Leading up to a challenging confrontation with enemy revenants in season 4, Wynonna turns to Nicole and asks if she wants to be Thelma or Louise.[9]

While it remains a powerful film for many viewers, there are aspects of *Thelma & Louise* that deserve careful scrutiny, including its relationship to settler fantasies of the West, its treatment of race and regional belonging, and its ambivalence about petrocultures and environmental destruction. By focusing on the movie's relevance while also attending to its limitations, we may note how *Thelma & Louise* introduces concerns about whiteness, racism, nation, and ecology that it does not resolve. Yet it is important for viewers to note how these concerns continue to shape discussions of the Western and to recognize the strategies that recent Western movies and TV shows have developed for engaging these problems.

Finally, it is useful to observe how the conversations that *Thelma & Louise* has generated over the years have often centered more on its female writer and leads than on its male director. Since it was first released, discussions about *Thelma & Louise* have tended to sideline the auteur and instead have focused on the women involved in other aspects of production. As such, the film provides a rare instance of women's achievements overshadowing those of men. While the auteur theory, or idea that the director is the creative force responsible for shaping a film, remains a popular concept in some circles, Karen Hollinger notes that it has been critiqued as subscribing to the "Great Man Theory of Film History" while ignoring the ways movies actually involve a process of collaboration with many people playing key roles. As she points out, the overemphasis on the achievements of directors largely favors the work of men, who have historically dominated the field, while marginalizing the contributions of women, who have tended to work in other areas of film production.[10]

The focus on the female director and the female leads in discussions of *Thelma & Louise* departs from the way movies, and particularly Westerns, are typically addressed. As such, these responses build on the powerful message that the movie expresses about extending the kind of stories told about the West and emphasizing the collective power of women's voices. While there is still much work to be done in the film industry regarding gender, sexuality, race, and equality, the impact and achievement of *Thelma & Louise* may be seen in how the movie helped foreground marginalized elements in the Western while popularizing new stories about power and agency. There are still political changes that need to be achieved, and we hope for new films that can offer inroads that may help us one day reach beyond the abyss, as Thelma and Louise themselves seek to do at the end of the movie.

# NOTES

## INTRODUCTION

1. For information on the film's budget and box office earnings, see the Internet Movie Database (IMDb), https://www.imdb.com/title/tt0103074/?ref_=fn_al_tt_1. The Writers Guild of America West posts its rankings of best screenplays at https://www.wga.org/writers-room/101-best-lists/101-greatest-screenplays/list. The American Film Institute lists its top heroes in cinema at https://www.afi.com/afis-100-years-100-heroes-villians/. (All websites accessed February 22, 2023.) For more on the film's Library of Congress induction, see D'Zurilla, "Susan Sarandon on 'Thelma & Louise.'" For a discussion of the proposed *Thelma & Louise* musical, see Gardner, "'Thelma & Louise' Screenwriter Developing Musical."

2. Nelson, "Hollywood Westerns," 331.

3. Nelson, "Introduction," xiv, xv; emphasis in original. He also points out that many of these recent Westerns have gained critical acclaim, winning Oscars and other major film awards. Since the 1990s, a shift in status has occurred. While the Western was once a popular genre, he notes that it may now be considered a "prestige" genre (xx).

4. Kaplan, "Rebel Citizenship," 20n10.

5. Aikman, *Off the Cliff*, 248.

6. Cook, "'Something's Crossed Over in Me,'" 25.

7. Here, I am indebted to Nora Gilbert's discussion, in her essay "'Impatient to Be Gone,'" of female mobility, transgression, and "unlawful escape" in women's literary histories.

8. For further discussion of genre hybridity, see Moine, *Cinema Genre*, 120.

9. Felski, *Hooked*, 97.

10. Felski, *Hooked*, 98.

11. A number of critics have addressed this point. See, for instance, Lamont, "Popular Western in Print"; Lamont, *Westerns*; Bold, *Frontier Club*; Tatum, "Problem of the 'Popular' in the New Western History"; Campbell, *Post-Westerns*; Nelson, *Still in the Saddle*; Mitchell, *Late Westerns*; Garrett-Davis, *What Is a Western?*; Frayling, *Spaghetti Westerns*; Higgins, Keresztesi, and Oscherwitz, eds., *The Western in the Global South*; Mayer and Roche, eds., *Transnationalism and Imperialism*.

## CHAPTER 1

1. Khouri, "Callie Khouri on *Thelma & Louise*," 98.

2. Khouri, "Callie Khouri on *Thelma & Louise*," 100.

3. Donnelly, "Pop Culture and Feminism"; Aikman, *Off the Cliff*, 248.

4. Frayling, "Mexico," 185.

5. Benson, "True or False."

6. Cook, "Women," 241.

7. Khouri, "Interview with Callie Khouri" (Burke), xiv.

8. Rosanne Welch offers an astute analysis of *The Wizard of Oz* that provides a different "hero's journey" for the female protagonist in the Western. For more on the argument, see Welch, "When Women Wrote Westerns."

9. Although the sequences are set in Arkansas, these elements remind us of the connections between the South and the West in Westerns such as *True Grit*, both the 1969 version (Henry Hathaway) and the 2010 remake (Ethan and Joel Coen), which also feature an avenging female character whose life is upended by violence.

10. Cook, "Women," 241.

11. Garrett-Davis, *What Is a Western?*, 49.

12. Garrett-Davis, *What Is a Western?*, 49, 3.

13. A number of critics have addressed phallic imagery in the film. See, for instance, Cook, "'Something's Crossed Over in Me,'" 15; Sturtevant, "Getting Hysterical," 48; Knobloch, "Interplaying Identities," 112. In *West of Everything*, Tompkins argues that the Western often "worships the phallus" (28) and that

the genre frequently centers on "empty spaces and lonely buttes" that "depict a phallic landscape of death" (28, 177).

14. Putnam, "The Bearer of the Gaze," 296.

15. For further discussion, see Buscombe, "Railroads," 205–9.

16. Murray and Heumann, *Gunfight at the Eco-Corral*, 143.

17. Rollins, "Tulsa (1949) as an Oil-Field Film," 83.

18. Sturken, *Thelma & Louise*, 36.

19. Sturken, *Thelma & Louise*, 36, 62.

20. Etulain, "Origins of the Western," 58.

21. Turner, "Significance of the Frontier in American History."

22. Khouri, "Interview with Callie Khouri" (Cook), 186.

23. Handley and Lewis, "Introduction," 1.

24. For more on this figure, see Lewis, *American Adam*, 5.

25. Anker, *Ugly Freedoms*, 2.

26. Anker, *Ugly Freedoms*, 6

27. Anker, *Ugly Freedoms*, 3.

28. Byrd, *Transit of Empire*, 221.

29. Anker, *Ugly Freedoms*, 18.

30. For further discussion of the film and the novel, see Kollin, "Race, Labor, and the Gothic Western."

31. Cristofani and Wertmüller codirected the film under the name Nathan Wich and cowrote the film under the pen name George Brown. For more on Wertmüller's career, see Pulver, "Lina Wertmüller." For more about the on-screen figure of Belle Starr, see Mock, "'My Body for a Hand of Poker,'" 171.

32. Mock, "'My Body for a Hand of Poker,'" 172.

33. Sturtevant, "Getting Hysterical," 43.

34. Chumo, "*Thelma & Louise* as Screwball Comedy," 24.

35. For more on screwball comedy Westerns, see Bingham, "'Before She Was a Virgin'"; Sickels, "'We're in a Tight Spot!'"; Samuels, *Northern Exposure*, 87. For a discussion of gender in the Western and the screwball comedy, see Haskell, *From Reverence to Rape*, 22, xix.

36. Rothman, "Screwball Comedy," 2, 11. See also Cavell, *Pursuits of Happiness*, 17, 122.

37. Rothman, "Screwball Comedy," 4 and 5.

38. Lenihan, "Westbound," 126.

39. Lenihan, "Westbound," 126.

40. Haskell, *From Reverence to Rape*, 137.

41. Fiedler, "Many Names of S. Levin," 125, 126, 127.

42. Griggers, "*Thelma and Louise*," 132, 133.

43. For additional discussions of this role reversal, see Sturken, *Thelma & Louise*, 51; Sturtevant, "Getting Hysterical," 48–49. Gender reversals are a common feature in screwball comedies; for further discussion of these reversals, see Shumway, "Screwball Comedies."

44. Sturken, *Thelma & Louise*, 48–49.

45. Ebert, "Thelma and Louise."

## CHAPTER 2

1. Willis, *High Contrast*, 99.

2. Leo, "Toxic Feminism," 192.

3. *Newsweek*, "Women Who Kill Too Much."

4. Carlson, "Is This What Feminism Is All About?," 57.

5. Khouri, "Callie Khouri on *Thelma & Louise*," 102.

6. Quoted in Spelman and Minow, "Outlaw Women," 264.

7. D'Zurilla, "Susan Sarandon on 'Thelma & Louise.'"

8. Khouri, "Callie Khouri on *Thelma & Louise*," 98.

9. Weller, "Ride of a Lifetime." The next year, Foster went on to win the Academy Award for best actress for the role of Clarice Starling, beating out both Geena Davis and Susan Sarandon for their work in *Thelma & Louise*.

10. See Weller, "Ride of a Lifetime."

11. In "What All the Fuss Is About," Fuchs suggests the reference is to James Dean (159). Meanwhile, LoBrutto offers "juvenile delinquent" in *Ridley Scott*, 97.

12. Weller, "Ride of a Lifetime," 5; Chang, "Gay for Brad," 205–6.

13. Taubin, "Ridley Scott's Road Work," 72, 76.

14. Taubin, "Ridley Scott's Road Work," 76. Also noting a similarity in the director's work, Johnson describes *Alien* and *Blade Runner* as "science-fiction quasi-Westerns" in *New Westers*, 236.

15. Upchurch, "Road Thrill."

16. Khouri, "Interview with Callie Khouri" (Cook), 169, 184.

17. Felski, *Hooked*, 99.

18. Simpson, "Moving into the Driver's Seat."

19. Baumgarten, "Thelma and Louise."

20. Maslin, "On the Road."

21. Dargis, "'Thelma & Louise,'" 86, 87.

22. Dargis, "'Thelma & Louise,'" 87, 89.

23. Dargis, "'Thelma & Louise,'" 90, 92.

24. Dargis, "'Thelma & Louise,'" 92.

25. Taubin, "Ridley Scott's Road Work," 78.

26. Khouri, "Interview with Callie Khouri" (Cook), 184, 186–87.

27. Khouri, "Callie Khouri on *Thelma & Louise*," 102.

28. Khouri, "Callie Khouri on *Thelma & Louise*," 104.

29. Comer, "Staying with the White Trouble," 104–5.

30. LoBrutto, *Ridley Scott*, 95.

31. Taubin, "Ridley Scott's Road Work," 77; Farry, "European Western."

32. D'Zurilla, "Susan Sarandon on 'Thelma & Louise.'"

33. Taubin, "Ridley Scott's Road Work," 77.

34. McDonagh, "*Thelma & Louise* Hit the Road," 73–74.

35. Taubin, "Ridley Scott's Road Work," 77.

36. LoBrutto, *Ridley Scott*, 95–96, 98.

37. LoBrutto, *Ridley Scott*, 96.

38. The audio commentary on the DVD of the film includes Khouri's discussion of *Lonely Are the Brave* as an inspiration; see also Khouri, "Interview with Callie Khouri" (Cook), 168.

39. Khouri, "Up Close with Callie Khouri," 90.

40. Khouri, "Up Close with Callie Khouri," 92.

41. Beauchamp, "Foreword," 1.

42. Will, "Nervous Origins of the Western."

43. Lamont, *Westerns*, 1.

44. Lamont, "Popular Western in Print," 102.

45. Lamont, *Westerns*, 155.

46. Lamont, "Popular Western in Print," 94.

47. Lamont, *Westerns*, 6.

48. Brown, "American Indian Modernities," 295.

49. For more on how women's narratives become classified as domestic fiction or sentimental literature, see Lamont, *Westerns*, 4.

50. Tompkins, *West of Everything*, 42.

51. Tompkins, *West of Everything*, 41.

52. Tompkins, *West of Everything*, 39.

53. Lamont, *Westerns*, 1–2.

54. Bold, *Frontier Club*, xvii.

55. Bold, *Frontier Club*, xviii, xvii.

56. Bold, *Frontier Club*, xix.

57. Bold, *Frontier Club*, xvii–xviii.

58. For more on this history, see Beauchamp, "Foreword," 1; Welch, "When Women Wrote Westerns."

59. McMahan, *Alice Guy Blaché*, xx, 133; Bold, "Early Cinematic Westerns," 228.

60. For more on the film, see Tevis, "Alice Guy Blaché's *Parson Sue*," 36–37.

61. For more on her biography, see McMahan, *Alice Guy Blaché*.

62. Beauchamp, "Foreword," 2.

63. Biographical information about Frances Marion is listed on IMDb at https://www.imdb.com/name/nm0547966/; see also Ruvoli, "Frances Marion."

64. Aikman, *Off the Cliff*, 268–69.

65. Bean, "Grace Cunard."

66. Cooper, "Ruth Ann Baldwin."

67. Armatage, *Girl from God's Country*, 98.

68. Mahar, *Women Filmmakers in Early Hollywood*, 2.

69. Francke, *Script Girls*, 74.

70. Mahar, *Women Filmmakers in Early Hollywood*, 2.

71. For a listing of Ida Lupino's work, see her entry on IMDb at https://www.imdb.com/name/nm0526946/?ref_=fn_al_nm_1. For Leah Brackett's credits, see her IMDb entry at https://www.imdb.com/name/nm0102824/?ref_=fn_al_nm_3. For Carole Eastman's credits, see the IMDb entry for *The Shootist* at https://www.imdb.com/title/tt0062262/?ref_=fn_al_tt_1. For Sonia

Chernus's credits, see her IMDb entry at https://www.imdb.com/name/ nm0155963/?ref_=fn_al_nm_1. (All accessed March 29, 2023.)

72. Matheson, "Introduction," 13.

73. For a useful overview of this history, see Deloria, *Indians in Unexpected Places*, 80.

74. For more on these refusals, see Moses, *Wild West Shows*, 234–37. Raheja recounts these stories in her analysis of "redfacing" in *Reservation Reelism*, 21.

75. Raheja, *Reservation Reelism*, 25; Bold, "Early Cinematic Westerns," 228.

76. Aleiss, *Making the White Man's Indian*, 2.

77. Raheja, *Reservation Reelism*, 59.

78. Aleiss, *Making the White Man's Indian*, 17.

79. This information is drawn from NWIFTV's website, https://www.native-womeninfilm.com, accessed 20 July 2022.

## CHAPTER 3

1. Slotkin, "Violence," 233.

2. Slotkin, "Violence," 233.

3. Mitchell, *Westerns*, 10.

4. Cawelti, *Six-Gun Mystique Sequel*, 55.

5. Khouri, "Interview with Callie Khouri" (Cook), 174, 183.

6. Francke, *Script Girls*, 132.

7. Kotsopoulos, "Gendering Expectations," 318.

8. Khouri, "Interview with Callie Khouri" (Burke), xiv.

9. Khouri, "Interview with Callie Khouri" (Cook), 171.

10. Khouri, "Interview with Callie Khouri" (Cook), 178.

11. Kitses, *Horizons West*, 256.

12. Buscombe, "Rape," 209.

13. Cook, "Women," 242.

14. For a discussion of how sexual violence operates in tandem with settler colonialism, see Deer, *Beginning and End of Rape*.

15. Arguing that the rape-revenge narrative was established in Westerns before it became associated with horror and other genres, Heller-Nicholas notes that films such as *Hannie Caulder* (1971) and *Jessi's Girls* (Al Adamson, 1975) draw

on the revenge plot of the Western described by Will Wright by featuring female characters who track down their rapists. For further discussion, see Heller-Nicholas, *Rape-Revenge Films*, 68, 70–71. Buscombe notes that while Westerns often center on rape and sexual violence, they frequently do not "examine the experience, or the consequences except in one respect: rape is the occasion for the outraged to seek revenge." See Buscombe, "Rape," 209.

16. For further discussion of how rape and honor are treated in the Western, see Coelho, "'We Been Haunted a Long Time,'" 193–94. In her study of rape-revenge Westerns, Read notes that the figure who seeks vengeance is typically a husband or fiancé rather than the woman who was raped. For further discussion, see Read, *New Avengers*, 125.

17. For Madsen's comments, see Aikman, *Off the Cliff*, 135.

18. Srinivasan, *Right to Sex*, 13. For an astute analysis of how women might somehow "lose" the right to consent, see Bundtzen, "*Thelma and Louise*," 179–81.

19. Srinivasan, *Right to Sex*, 21.

20. Srinivasan, *Right to Sex*, 21.

21. Buscombe, "Gunfighters," 132.

22. Buscombe, "Guns," 132.

23. Buscombe, "Guns," 132.

24. Nelson, "Hollywood Westerns," 338.

25. Wertmüller is frequently listed as a codirector of the film. She was initially hired in that capacity but was fired after only a few days on the job. See Heller-Nicholas, *Rape-Revenge Films*, 75, 153.

26. The BBC/Amazon miniseries *The English* (created by Hugo Blick, 2022) may be regarded as another Western with a female lead that is also influenced by the spaghetti Western.

27. Spivak, "Can the Subaltern Speak?," 76–77.

28. Fricker, *Epistemic Injustice*, 1, 3.

29. Abramson, "Turning Up the Lights," 2, 18.

30. Abramson, "Turning Up the Lights," 3.

31. Abramson, "Turning Up the Lights," 5, 6, 8.

32. Abramson, "Turning Up the Lights," 8.

33. Abramson, "Turning Up the Lights," 10.

34. Khouri, "Callie Khouri on *Thelma & Louise*," 100.

35. Abramson, "Turning Up the Lights," 12–13.

36. Abramson, "Turning Up the Lights," 15.

37. Manne, *Down Girl*, xiii.

38. Manne, *Down Girl*, xix, 87.

39. Manne, *Down Girl*, xix.

40. Srinivasan, "Aptness of Anger," 126.

41. Srinivasan, "Aptness of Anger," 126.

42. Srinivasan, "Aptness of Anger," 127.

43. Srinivasan, "Aptness of Anger," 128; emphasis in original.

44. Srinivasan, "Aptness of Anger," 129.

45. Srinivasan, "Aptness of Anger," 132.

46. Tasker, *Spectacular Bodies*, 150.

47. Tasker, *Spectacular Bodies*, 154.

48. Here I draw on Merriam-Webster's definition of *bitch*: "informal + often offensive: a malicious, spiteful, or overbearing woman" (https://www.merriam-webster.com/dictionary/bitch).

49. Sturken, *Thelma & Louise*, 38–39.

50. For a discussion of men and language in the Western, see Cawelti, *Six-Gun Mystique Sequel*, 41. For more on wordplay in the Western, see Mitchell, *Westerns*, 98–100.

51. Willis, *High Contrast*, 115.

52. Cook, "'Something's Crossed Over in Me,'" 29.

53. While Westerns sympathetic to the "Lost Cause" exist, *Thelma & Louise* uses the Confederate flag differently from those films. Still, one wishes that someone in production back in 1991 had stepped up. Yet there it is. We must acknowledge the problem and learn from it.

54. Goodman, *Planetary Lens*, 4.

55. See Spence, *Dispossessing the Wilderness*; Keller and Turek, *American Indians and National Parks*. Many of these tribal lands are now under the jurisdiction of the National Park Service. For more information, see National Park Service, "Exploring Tribal Connections to Arches National Park," accessed July 6, 2022, https://www.nps.gov/articles/arch-eoa.htm; National Park Service, "American Indians," accessed July 6, 2022, https://www.nps.gov/cany/learn/historyculture/nativeamericans.htm.

56. A number of scholars have written studies of the erasure and misrepresentation of Native Americans in cinema, as well as of films by Indigenous artists that counter these narratives. See, for instance, Aleiss, *Making the White Man's Indian* and "From the *Squaw Man* to *Rutherford Falls*"; Bold, "Early Cinematic Westerns"; Buscombe, *Injuns!*; Hearne, *Native Recognition*; Kilpatrick, *Celluloid Indians*; Rollins and O'Connor, eds., *Hollywood's Indian*; Singer, *Wiping the War Paint Off the Lens*; Raheja, *Reservation Reelism*.

57. Aikman, *Off the Cliff*, 198. For more on the atomic history of the region, see Davis, "Dead West"; Kuletz, *Tainted Desert*.

58. Putnam, "Bearer of the Gaze," 296.

59. Goldberg, "Extractive Masculinity," 197, 198.

60. Alaimo, *Exposed*, 95–96.

61. Colebrook, "We Have Always Been Post-Anthropocene," 400.

## CONCLUSION

1. "*Thelma & Louise* Wins Original Screenplay."

2. Garber, "*Thelma & Louise* Holds Up Well."

3. For more on the #MeToo movement, see Burke, *Unbound*.

4. Campbell, *Affective Critical Regionality*, 3.

5. Smelik, "Feminist Film Theory," 498. It's worth pointing out that *Desert Hearts* (Donna Deitch, 1985) predates *Thelma & Louise* and also queers desire in the Western in more detail.

6. For a discussion of the film's impact, see Handley, *Brokeback Book*, 2011. For information about the film's budget and box office returns, see the film's IMDb entry at https://www.imdb.com/title/tt0388795/?ref_=nv_sr_srsg_0

7. For information about the budget and box office returns, see the film's entry on IMDb at https://www.imdb.com/title/tt10293406/?ref_=fn_al_tt_1.

8. For more on this hybrid genre, see Fine, Johnson, Lush, and Spurgeon, eds., *Weird Westerns*.

9. For an astute analysis of the show, see Lush, "Racial Metaphors and Vanishing *indians*."

10. For further discussion of feminist critiques of the auteur theory, see Hollinger, *Feminist Film Studies*, 231.

# BIBLIOGRAPHY

## FILMOGRAPHY

*The Accused* (Jonathan Kaplan, 1988)

*Alien* (Ridley Scott, 1979)

*Badlands* (Terrence Malick, 1973)

*Bandidas* (Joachim Rønning and Espen Sandberg, 2006)

*The Belle Starr Story* (Piero Cristofani and Lina Wertmüller, 1968)

*Blade Runner* (Ridley Scott, 1982)

*Bonnie and Clyde* (Arthur Penn, 1967)

*Brokeback Mountain* (Ang Lee, 2005)

*Butch Cassidy and the Sundance Kid* (George Roy Hill, 1969)

*Dances with Wolves* (Kevin Costner, 1990)

*Desert Hearts* (Donna Deitch, 1985)

*Duel in the Sun* (King Vidor and Otto Brower, 1946)

*Easy Rider* (Dennis Hopper, 1969)

*The English* (created by Hugo Blick, 2022)

*Forty Guns* (Sam Fuller, 1957)

*'49–'17* (Ruth Ann Baldwin, 1917)

*Gaslight* (George Cukor, 1944)

*The Girl from God's Country* (Nell Shipman and Edmund Burns, 1921)

*Hannie Caulder* (Burt Kennedy, 1971)

*Jessi's Girls* (Al Adamson, 1975)

*Johnny Guitar* (Nicholas Ray, 1954)

*Lonely Are the Brave* (David Miller, 1962)

*The Outlaw Josey Wales* (Clint Eastwood, 1976)

*Parson Sue* (Alice Guy Blaché, 1912)

*The Power of the Dog* (Jane Campion, 2021)

*Promising Young Woman* (Emerald Fennell, 2020)

*The Searchers* (John Ford, 1956)

*Shane* (George Stevens, 1953)

*Smoke Signals* (Chris Eyre, 1998)

*Thelma & Louise* (Ridley Scott, 1991)

*Thousand Pieces of Gold* (Nancy Kelly, 1990)

*True Grit* (Henry Hathaway, 1969)

*True Grit* (Ethan and Joel Coen, 2010)

*Unbelievable* (created by Susannah Grant, Ayelet Waldman, and Michael Chabon, 2019)

*The Virginian* (Victor Fleming, 1929)

*The Wind* (Victor Sjöström, 1928)

*The Wizard of Oz* (Victor Fleming, 1939)

*Wynonna Earp* (created by Emily Andras, 2016–2021)

## BOOKS AND ARTICLES

Abramson, Kate. "Turning up the Lights on Gaslighting." *Philosophical Perspectives* 28 (2014): 1–30.

Aikman, Becky. *Off the Cliff: How the Making of Thelma & Louise Drove Hollywood to the Edge*. New York: Penguin, 2017.

Alaimo, Stacy. *Exposed: Environmental Politics and Pleasures in Posthuman Times*. Minneapolis: University of Minnesota Press, 2016.

Aleiss, Angela. "From the *Squaw Man* to *Rutherford Falls*: The Rise of Hollywood's Contemporary Native American Woman." *Bright Lights Film Journal*, August 5, 2021. https://brightlightsfilm.com/from-the-squaw-man-to-rutherford-falls-the-rise-of-hollywoods-contemporary-native-american-woman/#.Ytby2-zMKCS.

———. *Making the White Man's Indian: Native Americans and Hollywood Movies*. Westport, CT: Praeger, 2005.

Anker, Elizabeth R. *Ugly Freedoms*. Durham, NC: Duke University Press, 2022.

Armatage, Kay. *The Girl from God's Country: Nell Shipman and the Silent Cinema*. Toronto: University of Toronto Press, 2003.

Baumgarten, Marjorie. "Thelma and Louise." *Austin Chronicle*, May 24, 1991. https://www.austinchronicle.com/events/film/1991-05-24/thelma-and-louise/.

Bean, Jennifer M. "Grace Cunard." Women Film Pioneers Project, edited by Jane Gaines, Radha Vatsal, and Monica Dall'Asta. Columbia University Libraries, 2013. https://doi.org/10.7916/d8-zpaq-rp55.

Beauchamp, Cari. "Foreword: Finding Frances Marion." In *When Women Wrote Hollywood: Essays on Screenwriters in the Early Film Industry*, edited by Rosanne Welch, 1–4. Jefferson, NC: McFarland, 2018.

Benson, Sheila. "True or False: Thelma and Louise Just Good Ole Boys?" *Los Angeles Times*, May 31, 1991. https://www.latimes.com/archives/la-xpm-1991-05-31-ca-2730-story.html.

Bingham, Dennis. "'Before She Was a Virgin . . .': Doris Day and the Decline of Female Film Comedy in the 1950s and 1960s." *Cinema Journal* 45, no. 3 (2006): 3–31.

Bold, Christine. "Early Cinematic Westerns." In *A History of Western American Literature*, edited by Susan Kollin, 225–41. Cambridge: Cambridge University Press, 2015.

———. *The Frontier Club: Popular Westerns and Cultural Power, 1880–1924*. Oxford: Oxford University Press, 2013.

Brown, Kirby. "American Indian Modernities and New Modernist Studies' Indian Problem." *Texas Studies in Language and Literature* 59, no. 3 (2017): 287–318.

Bundtzen, Lynda K. "*Thelma and Louise*: A Story Not to Be Believed." *Communication Review* 1, no. 2 (1995): 179–200.

Burke, Tarana. *Unbound: My Story of Liberation and the Birth of the Me Too Movement*. New York: Flatiron Press, 2021.

Buscombe, Edward. "Gunfighters." In *The BFI Companion to the Western*, edited by Edward Buscombe, 132. New York: DaCapo Press, 1988.

———. "Guns." In *The BFI Companion to the Western*, edited by Edward Buscombe, 132. New York: DaCapo Press, 1988.

———. *Injuns! Native Americans in the Movies*. New York: Reaktion Books, 2012.

———. "Railroads." In *The BFI Companion to the Western*, edited by Edward Buscombe, 205–9. New York: DaCapo Press, 1988.

———. "Rape." In *The BFI Companion to the Western*, edited by Edward Buscombe, 209. New York: DaCapo Press, 1988.

Byrd, Jodi. *The Transit of Empire: Indigenous Critiques of Colonialism*. Minneapolis: University of Minnesota Press, 2011.

Campbell, Neil. *Affective Critical Regionality*. London: Rowman and Littlefield International, 2016.

———. *Post-Westerns: Cinema, Region, West*. Lincoln: University of Nebraska Press, 2013.

Carlson, Margaret. "Is This What Feminism Is All About?" *Time*, June 24, 1991, 57.

Cavell, Stanley. *Pursuits of Happiness: The Hollywood Comedy of Remarriage*. Cambridge, MA: Harvard University Press, 1981.

Cawelti, John. *The Six-Gun Mystique Sequel*. Bowling Green: The Popular Press / Bowling Green State University Press, 1999.

Chang, Edmond Y. "Gay for Brad." *Deconstructing Brad Pitt*, edited by Christopher Schaberg and Robert Bennett, 204–12. New York: Bloomsbury, 2014.

Chumo, Peter N., II. "*Thelma & Louise* as Screwball Comedy." *Film Quarterly* 24, no. 2 (Winter 1991–1992): 548–50.

Coelho, Cecilía de Miranda N. "'We Been Haunted a Long Time'—Raped Women in Westerns." In *Women in the Western*, edited by Sue Mathison, 187–200. Edinburgh: Edinburgh University Press, 2020.

Colebrook, Claire. "We Have Always Been Post-Anthropocene: The Anthropocene Counterfactual." In *Energy Humanities: An Anthology*, edited by Imre Szeman and Dominic Boyer, 399–414. Baltimore: Johns Hopkins University Press, 2017.

Comer, Krista. "Staying with the White Trouble of Recent Feminist Westerns." *Western American Literature* 56, no. 2 (Summer 2021): 101–23.

Cook, Bernie. "'Something's Crossed Over in Me': New Ways of Seeing *Thelma & Louise*." In *Thelma & Louise Live! The Cultural Afterlife of an American Film*, edited by Bernie Cook, 7–42. Austin: University of Texas Press, 2007.

Cook, Pam. "Women." In *The BFI Companion to the Western*, edited by Edward Buscombe, 240–43. New York: Da Capo Press, 1988.

Cooper, Mark Garrett. "Ruth Ann Baldwin." Women Film Pioneers Project, edited by Jane Gaines, Radha Vatsal, and Monica Dall'Asta. Columbia University Libraries, 2013. https://doi.org/10.7916/d8-09tg-1y17.

Dargis, Manohla. "'Thelma & Louise' and the Tradition of the Male Road Movie." In *Women and Film: A Sight and Sound Reader*, edited by Pam Cook and Philip Dodd, 86–92. Philadelphia: Temple University Press, 1993.

Davis, Mike. "Dead West: Ecocide in Marlboro Country." In *Over the Edge: Remapping the American West*, edited by Valerie J. Matsumoto and Blake Allmendinger, 339–69. Berkeley: University of California Press, 1999.

Deer, Sarah. *The Beginning and End of Rape: Confronting Sexual Violence in Native America*. Minneapolis: University of Minnesota Press, 2015.

Deloria, Phil. *Indians in Unexpected Places*. Lawrence: University Press of Kansas, 2004.

Donnelly, Liza. "Pop Culture and Feminism: An Interview with Hollywood's Callie Khouri." *Forbes*, February 26, 2014. https://www.forbes.com/sites/lizadonnelly/2014/02/26/pop-culture-and-feminism-an-interview-with-hollywoods-callie-khouri/?sh=15cf36f01ac1.

D'Zurilla, Christie. "Susan Sarandon on 'Thelma & Louise': We Didn't Set Out to Make a Feminist Film." *Los Angeles Times*, December 14, 2016. https://www.latimes.com/entertainment/gossip/la-et-mg-susan-sarandon-thelma-louise-national-film-registry-20161214-story.html.

Ebert, Roger. "Thelma and Louise." January 1, 1991. https://www.rogerebert.com/reviews/thelma-and-louise-1991.

Etulain, Richard. "Origins of the Western." In *Critical Essays on the Western Novel*, edited by William J. Pilkington, 56–60. Boston: G. K. Hall, 1980.

Farry, Oliver. "The European Western: Popular Culture for the Late Imperial Age." *New Statesman*, September 24, 2014. https://www.newstatesman.com/culture/2014/09/european-western-popular-culture-late-imperial-age.

Felski, Rita. *Hooked: Art and Attachment*. Chicago: University of Chicago Press, 2020.

Fiedler, Leslie. "The Many Names of S. Levin: An Essay in Genre Criticism." In *Fiedler on the Roof: Essays on Literature and Jewish Identity*, edited by Leslie Fiedler, 123–38. New York: David R. Godine Publisher, 1991.

Fine, Kerry, Michael K. Johnson, Rebecca Lush, and Sara L. Spurgeon, eds. *Weird Westerns: Race, Gender, Genre*. Lincoln: University of Nebraska Press, 2020.

Francke, Lizzie. *Script Girls: Women Screenwriters in Hollywood*. London: BFI Press, 1994.

Frayling, Christopher. "Mexico." In *The BFI Companion to the Western*, edited by Edward Buscombe, 184–88. New York: Da Capo Press, 1988.

———. *Spaghetti Westerns: Cowboys and Europeans from Karl May to Sergio Leone*. 2nd ed. London: I. B. Tauris, 2006.

Fricker, Miranda. *Epistemic Injustice: Power and the Ethics of Knowing*. Oxford: Oxford University Press, 2007.

Fuchs, Cynthia. "What All the Fuss Is About: Making Brad Pitt in *Thelma & Louise*." In *Thelma & Louise Live! The Cultural Aftermath of an American Film*, edited by Bernie Cook, 146–67. Austin: University of Texas Press, 2007.

Garber, Megan. "*Thelma & Louise* Holds Up Well—A Little Too Well." *Atlantic*, May 24, 2016. https://www.theatlantic.com/entertainment/archive/2016/05/thelma-louise-holds-up-wella-little-too-well/484121/.

Gardner, Chris. "'Thelma & Louise' Screenwriter Developing Musical Based on 1991 Film: 'It's Very Promising.'" *Hollywood Reporter*, June 22, 2021. https://www.hollywoodreporter.com/movies/movie-news/thelma-and-louise-musical-1234971756/.

Garrett-Davis, Josh. *What Is a Western? Region, Genre, Imagination*. Norman: University of Oklahoma Press, 2019.

Gilbert, Nora. "'Impatient to Be Gone': Aphra Behn's Vindication of the Flights of Women." *Eighteenth-Century Life* 4, no. 1 (January 2018): 1–27.

Goldberg, Sylvan. "Extractive Masculinity: The Western's Precarious Male

Bodies in the Anthropocene." In *The Routledge Companion to Gender and the American West*, edited by Susan Bernardin, 197–209. New York: Routledge, 2022.

Goodman, Audrey. *A Planetary Lens: The Photo-Poetics of Western Women's Writing*. Lincoln: University of Nebraska Press, 2021.

Griggers, Cathy. "*Thelma and Louise* and the Cultural Generation of the New Butch-Femme." In *Film Theory Goes to the Movies*, edited by Hilary Radner, 129–41. New York: Routledge, 1993.

Handley, William R, ed. *The Brokeback Book: From Story to Cultural Phenomenon*. Lincoln: University of Nebraska Press, 2011.

Handley, William R., and Nathaniel Lewis. "Introduction." In *True West: Authenticity and the American West*, edited by William R. Handley and Nathaniel Lewis, 1–17. Lincoln: University of Nebraska Press, 2003.

Haskell, Molly. *From Reverence to Rape: The Treatment of Women in the Movies*. New York: Penguin, 1973.

Hearne, Joanne. *Native Recognition: Indigenous Cinema and the Western*. New York: SUNY Press, 2012.

Heller-Nicholas, Alexandra. *Rape-Revenge Films: A Critical Study*. 2nd ed. Jefferson, NC: McFarland, 2021.

Higgens, MaryEllen, Rita Keresztesi, and Dana Oscherwitz, eds. *The Western in the Global South*. New York: Routledge, 2015.

Hollinger, Karen. *Feminist Film Studies*. New York: Routledge, 2012.

Johnson, Michael L. *New Westers: The West in Contemporary American Culture*. Lawrence: University Press of Kansas, 1996.

Kaplan, Michael. "Rebel Citizenship and the Cunning of the Liberal Imaginary in *Thelma & Louise*." *Communication and Critical/Cultural Studies* 5, no. 1 (2008): 1–23.

Keller, Robert H., and Michael F. Turek. *American Indians and National Parks*. Tucson: University of Arizona Press, 1999.

Khouri, Callie. "Callie Khouri on *Thelma & Louise*." In *On Story: Screenwriters and Filmmakers on Their Iconic Films*, edited by Barbara Morgan and Maya Perez, 98–104. Austin: University of Texas Press, 2016.

———. "An Interview with Callie Khouri." By Jodie Burke. In *Thelma & Louise and Something to Talk About: Screenplays*, Callie Khouri, vii–xxiv. New York: Grove Press, 1996.

———. "Interview with Callie Khouri." By Bernie Cook. In *Thelma & Louise Live! The Cultural Afterlife of an American Film*, edited by Bernie Cook, 168–89. Austin: University of Texas Press, 2007.

———. "Up Close with Callie Khouri." In *On Story: Screenwriters and Filmmakers on Their Iconic Films*, edited by Barbara Morgan and Maya Perez, 89–97. Austin: University of Texas Press, 2016.

Kilpatrick, Jacqueline. *Celluloid Indians: Native Americans and Film*. Lincoln: University of Nebraska Press, 1999.

Kitses, Jim. *Horizons West: Directing the Western from John Ford to Clint Eastwood*. 2nd ed. London: BFI Press, 2007.

Knobloch, Susan. "Interplaying Identities: Acting and the Building Blocks of Character in *Thelma & Louise*." In *Thelma & Louise Live! The Cultural Afterlife of an American Film*, edited by Bernie Cook, 91–121. Austin: University of Texas Press, 2007.

Kollin, Susan. "Race, Labor, and the Gothic Western: Dispelling Frontier Myths in Dorothy Scarborough's *The Wind*." *Modern Fiction Studies* 46, no. 3 (2000): 675–94.

Kotsopoulos, Aspasia. "Gendering Expectations: Genre and Allegory in Readings of *Thelma and Louise*." In *Hollywood's America: Twentieth-Century America Through Film*, edited by Steve Mintz and Randy Roberts, 309–28. Malden, MA: Wiley-Blackwell, 2010.

Kuletz, Valerie L. *Tainted Desert: Environmental and Social Ruin in the American West*. New York: Routledge, 1998.

Lamont, Victoria. "The Popular Western in Print: A Feminist Genealogy." In *The Routledge Companion to Gender and the American West*, edited by Susan Bernardin, 93–104. New York: Routledge, 2022.

———. *Westerns: A Women's History*. Lincoln: University of Nebraska Press, 2016.

Lenihan, John H. "Westbound: Feature Films and the American West." In *Wanted Dead or Alive: The American West in Popular Culture*, edited by Richard Aquila, 109–34. Champaign: University of Illinois Press, 1996.

Leo, John. "Toxic Feminism on the Big Screen." In *Thelma & Louise Live! Cultural Aftermath of an American Film*, edited by Bernie Cook, 191–93. Austin: University of Texas Press, 2007.

Lewis, R. W. B. *The American Adam: Innocence, Tragedy, and Tradition in the Nineteenth Century*. Chicago: University of Chicago Press, 1959.

LoBrutto, Vincent. *Ridley Scott: A Biography*. Lexington: University of Kentucky Press, 2019.

Lush, Rebecca. "Racial Metaphors and Vanishing *indians* in *Wynonna Earp*, *Buffy the Vampire Slayer*, and Emma Bull's *Territory*." In *Weird Westerns: Race, Gender, Genre*, edited by Kerry Fine, Michael K. Johnson, Rebecca Lush, and Sara L. Spurgeon, 255–88. Lincoln: University of Nebraska Press, 2020.

Mahar, Karen Ward. *Women Filmmakers in Early Hollywood*. Baltimore: Johns Hopkins University Press, 2006.

Manne, Kate. *Down Girl: The Logic of Misogyny*. Oxford: Oxford University Press, 2017.

Maslin, Janet. "On the Road with 2 Buddies and a Gun." *New York Times*, May 24, 1991. https://www.nytimes.com/1991/05/24/movies/review-film-on-the-run-with-2-buddies-and-a-gun.html.

Matheson, Sue. "Introduction." *Women in the Western*, edited by Sue Matheson, 1–8. Edinburgh: Edinburgh University Press, 2020.

Mayer, Hervé, and David Roche, eds. *Transnationalism and Imperialism: Endurance of the Global Western Film*. Bloomington: Indiana University Press, 2022.

McDonagh, Maitland. "Thelma & Louise Hit the Road for Ridley Scott." In *Ridley Scott: Interviews*, edited by Laurence F. Knapp and Andrea F. Kulas, 70–74. Jackson: University of Mississippi Press, 2005.

McMahan, Alison. *Alice Guy Blaché: Lost Visionary of the Cinema*. New York: Bloomsbury Press, 2002.

———. "Alice Guy Blaché." Women Film Pioneers Project, edited by Jane Gaines, Radha Vatsal, and Monica Dall'Asta. Columbia University Libraries, 2013. https://doi.org/10.7916/d8-5a4c-yq24.

Mitchell, Lee Clark. *Late Westerns: The Persistence of a Genre*. Lincoln: University of Nebraska Press, 2018.

———. *Westerns: Making the Man in Fiction and Film*. Chicago: University of Chicago Press, 1996.

Mock, Erin Lee. "'My Body for a Hand of Poker': *The Belle Starr Story* in Its Contexts." In *Women in the Western*, edited by Sue Matheson, 201–22. Edinburgh: University of Edinburgh Press, 2020. https://ebookcentral. proquest.com/lib/montana/reader.action?docID=6265429.

Moine, Raphaëlle. *Cinema Genre*. Translated by Alistair Fox and Hilary Radner. Malden, MA: Blackwell, 2008.

Morgan, Barbara, and Maya Perez, eds. *On Story: Screenwriters and Filmmakers on Their Iconic Films*. Austin: University of Texas Press, 2016.

Moses, L. G. *Wild West Shows and the Images of American Indians, 1883–1933*. Albuquerque: University of New Mexico Press, 1996.

Murray, Robin L., and Joseph K. Heumann. *Gunfight at the Eco-Corral: Western Cinema and the Environment*. Norman: University of Oklahoma Press, 2021.

Nelson, Andrew Patrick. "Hollywood Westerns: 1930 to the Present." In *A History of Western American Literature*, edited by Susan Kollin, 331–44. Cambridge: Cambridge University Press, 2015.

———. "Introduction: The American Western, 1990–2010." In *Contemporary Westerns: Film and Television Since 1990*, edited by Andrew Patrick Nelson, xiii–xxi. Lanham, MD: Rowman and Littlefield, 2013.

———. *Still in the Saddle: The Hollywood Western, 1969–1980*. Norman: University of Oklahoma Press, 2016.

*Newsweek*. "Women Who Kill Too Much." June 6, 1991. https://www.newsweek. com/women-who-kill-too-much-204418.

Pulver, Andrew. "Lina Wertmüller, First Woman to Be Nominated for Best Director Oscar, Dies Aged 93." *Guardian*, December 9, 2021. https:// www.theguardian.com/film/2021/dec/09/lina-wertmuller-first- woman-to-be-nominated-for-best-director-oscar-has-died-aged-93.

———. "Thelma & Louise Stage Musical in the Works." *Guardian*, June 23, 2021. https://www.theguardian.com/film/2021/jun/23/thelma-louise- stage-musical-in-the-works.

Putnam, Ann. "The Bearer of the Gaze in Ridley Scott's *Thelma and Louise*." *Western American Literature*, 27, no. 4 (Winter 1993): 291–302.

Raheja, Michelle. *Reservation Reelism: Redfacing, Visual Sovereignty, and Representations of Native Americans in Film*. Lincoln: University of Nebraska Press, 2010.

Read, Jacinda. *The New Avengers: Feminism, Femininity, and the Rape-Revenge Cycle*. Boston: St. Martin's Press, 2000.

Rollins, Peter. "*Tulsa* (1949) as an Oil-Field Film: A Study in Ecological Ambivalence." In *The Landscape of Hollywood Westerns: Ecocriticism in an American Film Genre*, edited by Deborah A. Carmichael, 81–93. Salt Lake City: University of Utah Press, 2006.

Rollins, Peter C., and John E. O'Connor, eds. *Hollywood's Indian: The Portrayal of the Native American in Film*. Lexington: University Press of Kentucky, 2003.

Rothman, William. "The Screwball Comedy." In *The Wiley-Blackwell History of American Film*, edited by Cynthia Lucia, Roy Grundmann, and Art Simon, 226–46. Malden, MA: Wiley-Blackwell, 2011. https://onlinelibrary.wiley.com/doi/full/10.1002/9780470671153.wbhaf030.

Ruvoli, JoAnne. "Frances Marion." Women Film Pioneers Project, edited by Jane Gaines, Radha Vatsal, and Monica Dall'Asta. Columbia University Libraries, 2013. https://doi.org/10.7916/d8-kvq5-gm17.

Samuels, Michael. *Northern Exposure: A Cultural History*. Lanham, MA: Rowman and Littlefield, 2021.

Schaberg, Christopher, and Robert Bennett, eds. *Deconstructing Brad Pitt*. New York: Bloomsbury Press, 2014.

Shumway, David R. "Screwball Comedies: Constructing Romance, Mystifying Marriage." *Cinema Journal* 30, no. 4 (Summer 1991): 7–23.

Sickels, Robert. "'We're in a Tight Spot!': The Coen Brothers' Screwy Romantic Comedies." *Journal of Popular Film and Television* 36, no. 3 (Fall 2008): 114–22.

Simpson, Janine C. "Moving into the Driver's Seat." *Time*, June 24, 1991. https://content.time.com/time/subscriber/article/0,33009,973249,00.html.

Singer, Beverly. *Wiping the War Paint Off the Lens: Native American Film and Video*. Minneapolis: University of Minnesota Press, 2001.

Slotkin, Richard. "Violence." In *The BFI Companion to the Western*, edited by
    Edward Buscombe, 232–36. New York: DaCapo Press, 1988.

Smelik, Anneke. "Feminist Film Theory." In *The Cinema Book*, 3rd ed., edited by
    Pam Cook, 491–504. New York: BFI Press, 2007.

Spellman, Elizabeth V., and Martha Minow. "Outlaw Women: *Thelma and
    Louise*." In *Legal Reelism: Movies as Legal Texts*, edited by John Denvir,
    261–79. Champaign: University of Illinois Press, 1996.

Spence, Mark David. *Dispossessing the Wilderness: Indian Removal and the Mak-
    ing of the National Parks*. Oxford: Oxford University Press, 1999.

Spivak, Gayatri. "Can the Subaltern Speak?" In *Colonial Discourse and Postcolo-
    nial Theory: A Reader*, edited by Patrick Williams and Laura Chrisman,
    66–111. New York: Columbia University Press, 1994.

Srinivasan. Amia. "The Aptness of Anger." *Journal of Political Philosophy* 26 no.
    2 (2018): 123–44.

Srinivasan, Amia. *The Right to Sex: Feminism in the Twenty-First Century*. New
    York: Farrar, Straus and Giroux, 2021.

Sturken, Marita. *Thelma & Louise*. London: British Film Institute, 2020.

Sturtevant, Victoria. "Getting Hysterical: *Thelma & Louise* and Laughter." In
    *Thelma & Louise Live! The Cultural Aftermath of an American Film*,
    edited by Bernie Cook, 43–64. Austin: University of Texas Press, 2007.

Tasker, Yvonne. *Spectacular Bodies: Gender, Genre, and the Action Cinema*. New
    York: Routledge, 1993.

Tatum, Stephen. "The Problem of the 'Popular' in the New Western History."
    *Arizona Quarterly* 53, no. 2 (Summer 1997): 153–90.

Taubin, Amy. "Ridley Scott's Road Work (1991)." In *Ridley Scott: Interviews*,
    edited by Lawrence F. Knapp and Andrea F. Kulas, 75–80. Jackson:
    University Press of Mississippi, 2005.

Tevis, Robert E. "Alice Guy Blaché's *Parson Sue*." *Classic Images* 468 (June 2014):
    36–37.

"*Thelma & Louise* Wins Original Screenplay: 1992 Oscars." Oscars. November 6,
    2013. YouTube video, 3:01. www.youtube.com/watch?v=29ePCxCBZ14.

Tompkins, Jane. *West of Everything: The Inner Life of Westerns*. New York:
    Oxford University Press, 1992.

Turner, Frederick Jackson. "The Significance of the Frontier in American History." In *The Frontier in American History*, 1–38. New York: Holt, Rinehart, and Winston, 1947. Reprint, Tucson: University of Arizona Press, 1986. Citations refer to University of Arizona Press edition.

Upchurch, Michael. "Road Thrill: Take a Wild Ride with 'Thelma and Louise.'" *Seattle Times*, May 24, 1991. https://archive.seattletimes.com/archive/?date=19910524&slug=1285157.

Welch, Rosanne. "When Women Wrote Westerns." What Is a Western? Interview Series, hosted by Josh Garrett-Davis, January 23, 2021. Video, 26:28. https://rosannewelch.com/2021/01/23/watch-dr-rosanne-welch-on-what-is-a-western-interview-series-when-women-wrote-westerns-from-the-autry-museum-of-the-american-west-video-27-minutes/.

Weller, Sheila. "The Ride of a Lifetime." *Vanity Fair*, March 3, 2011. https://archive.vanityfair.com/article/2011/3/the-ride-of-a-lifetime.

Will, Barbara. "The Nervous Origins of the Western." *American Literature* 70, no. 2 (June 1998): 293–316.

Willis, Sharon. *High Contrast: Race and Gender in Contemporary Hollywood Film*. Durham: Duke University Press, 1997.